T0204704

THE QUR'AN

Volume I: Surahs 1–3

Translation offered by
Camille Adams Helminski

First edition published 2023
by Threshold Books

Paperback ISBN: 978-0-939660-54-4
E-book ISBN: 978-0-939660-55-1

Library of Congress Control Number: 2023933347

Threshold Books
Escondido, London, Istanbul

www.sufism.org

Table of Contents

Preface
The Blessings of the Qur'an

Numerous keys are available to us to open the deeper meaning that lives within us; the words of the Holy Qur'an are such keys. The original Arabic resonances bestow grace through portals of expansive meaning, and even in translation some of the inherent blessing can be known. We offer here a journey with these meanings. We especially wish to thank Mahmoud Mostafa and Amira Abd El-Khalek, early readers of this text, for their insightful assistance, and dear Hamida Battla for her continual encouragement, and all the dear friends who have supported the unfoldings of this endeavor with their love.

Please note that within this text, each paragraph indent indicates a new verse (*ayah*, "sign"). And throughout, the word indicating "God," *Allah*, will be translated sometimes as "God" and sometimes as "Divine Reality," to remind us not to constrict our view but recognize the Infinitude of the Divine Reality we sometimes may speak of as "God." Likewise for related pronouns, sometimes "He," or "He/She" or "It" may be used in order to stretch our comprehension. All words in Arabic have a gender grammatically ascribed to them as they do in French and Spanish, etc. Although *Allah* is referred to with the third person masculine pronoun *Hu* (*Huwa*), it is universally understood that *Allah's* Essence is beyond gender or indeed any qualification. In this translation occasionally *Hu* will be used and sometimes "He/She" or "It" in an attempt to avoid the mistake of attributing human gender to That which is beyond all our attempts at definition, limitless in subtle glory.

When we are struck by the Lightning of Love during storms of intense grace, or when a key is provided to open an inner doorway for Divine Grace—that through which our own intrinsic spirit was formed—meanings may pour forth from within us, nourishing us afresh. We are not merely a molded substance of earth and water and synapses, but palpable beings of heart divined by the Eternal Spirit from which we were created. We know more than we know.

As Shams of Tabriz, the beloved mentor of Jalaluddin Rumi has said, "the Qur'an is a love-letter." May it continue to be, as it has been for many centuries, of blessed companionship, an opening towards Divine Reality, for all who approach it with an open heart.

May it be love!

With love,
Camille

Introduction

Volume I

Bismillah ar-Rahman ar-Rahim

We begin with the Name of God, the Infinitely Compassionate and Infinitely Merciful, with the seven oft-repeated verses of the *Fatiha*, "The Opening," offered through the heart of the Prophet Muhammad as a continual companion and guidance and love, from our Infinitely Compassionate and Continually Merciful Source.

Through his heart, may great peace and blessing be upon him, an intensive communication opened while in retreat he sought to connect more and more deeply with the Source of Being. When this communication began in the early years of the seventh century, he had already been among the *hanif*, those seeking to turn away from all that is false and to affirm Truth and to be guided to right action, following in the footsteps of Prophet Abraham. We remember well the story of how, in his cave of retreat on Mt. Hira, Muhammad felt the intense compression of the embrace of the angel Gabriel as the first words burst through his consciousness.[1] The words of the Qur'an were then revealed, unfolding over twenty-three

---

[1] See Preface and Introduction to *The Light of Dawn: Daily Readings from the Holy Qur'an*, Shambhala, 2000: pp. viii–xvi; pp. xx–xl.

years, step by step, while he witnessed the needs of his developing community, as guidance and Light for those who were hearing this Message of Divine Reality—as a *guidance for humanity*[2] and for *all the worlds*.[3] Through its guidance, respect for the natural world, for women, for orphans, for every human being, was encouraged. Women were granted more rights than in most other societies for many centuries to come; class exploitation diminished. A spiritual and social transformation occurred and continued to spread. Though the shorter *surahs* (chapters of verses or "signs," *ayat*)—many witnessing to the miracles of nature and all we have to learn from observing this amazing creation—were among the first to be conveyed, when the completed Qur'an was formed under Muhammad's counsel, before his passing, the longer *surahs* which include more particular ethical guidance for the emerging community and for humanity as a whole were placed at the fore. And so we begin here with the first three *surahs* of the traditional order of the Qur'an—*Surah al-Fatiha, Surah al-Baqarah*, and *Surah Al-'Imran*—which convey the principles of human ethics and the caution to remember that there are repercussions for all our actions and intentions, with the encouragement to turn again and again to realignment with our Source:

> *God—there is no deity but Hu, the Ever-Living,*
> *the Self-Subsistent, Eternal Source of All Being.*
> [*Allahu, la illaha illa Huwa, al-Hayy, al-Qayyum.*]
>
> [Qur'an, *Surah Al-'Imran* 3:2]

---

[2] Qur'an, *Surah al-Baqarah* 2:185.
[3] Qur'an, *Surah Sad* 38:87.

We are reminded through the Qur'an that the All-Knowing, Life-Giving Source of Sustenance and Guidance is never-tiring, continually communicating, sharing guidance and Love.

Step by step it is He/She who has sent down to you this Book,
within Truth, confirming what remains of earlier Revelation;
for it is He/She who bestowed the Torah and the Gospel,
before, as a guidance to humankind—
it is He/She who has sent down the criterion
for discerning right from wrong.

[Qur'an, *Surah Al-'Imran* 3:3]

God loves those who strive to act with beauty and goodness.

[Qur'an, *Surah Al-'Imran* 3:148]

God—there is no deity but "Hu," the Ever-Living,
the Self-Subsisting Source of all Being.
No slumber can seize Him/Her nor sleep.
All things in heaven and on earth belong to Hu.
Who could intercede in His/Her Presence
without His/Her permission?
He/She knows what appears in front of
and behind His/Her creatures.
Nor can they encompass any knowledge of Him/Her
except what He/She wills.
His/Her throne extends over the heavens and the earth,
and He/She feels no fatigue in guarding and preserving them,
for He/She is the Highest and Most Exalted.
Let there be no compulsion in matters of faith.
Right wayfaring stands clearly apart from error.
Whoever turns away from the powers of evil
and has faith in Divine Reality

has grasped the most trustworthy handhold
which shall never give way.
And Divine Reality is All-Hearing, All-Knowing.
Divine Reality is the Protector of those who have faith,
leading them out of the depths of darkness into the Light.

[Qur'an, *Surah al-Baqarah* 255 ("The Throne Verse")
and 256–257]

Sometimes the voice of the Qur'an comes to us speaking of the Divine Reality in the third person as in the preceding verses and many others such as:

O you who have faith,
seek help through steadfast patience and prayer,
for God is with those who patiently persevere.

[Qur'an, *Surah al-Baqarah* 2:153]

Sometimes, even in an adjacent verse, it comes through in the first person:

Remember Me—and I remember you.
And give thanks; do not turn away with ingratitude.

[Qur'an, *Surah al-Baqarah* 2:152]

And if My servants ask you about Me—truly, I am near.
I respond to the one who calls Me whenever he or she calls Me;
let them then respond to Me, and trust in Me,
that they might follow the well-guided way.

[Qur'an, *Surah al-Baqarah* 2:186]

I am the Acceptor of Repentance, Oft Re-Turning,
the Continually Merciful.

[Qur'an, *Surah al-Baqarah* 2:160]

And in other moments, it speaks to us as a collective "We":

> *O you who have faith, partake of the wholesome things*
> *that We have provided for you as sustenance.*

[Qur'an, *Surah al-Baqarah* 2:172]

Some have understood this "We" as the collective of the attributes or "Names" of God, *Al Asma al-Husna*, "The Most Beautiful Names," all the attributes of perfection, the qualities of the Divine that manifest throughout this creation in all their interplay and assist us in coming to know that Truth of Compassion and Mercy. The root word in Arabic for both "Compassion" (*Rahman*) and "Mercy" (*Rahim*), is the triliteral root word for "womb," and all but one of the *surahs* of the Qur'an begin with the phrase, *In the Name of God, the Infinitely Compassionate and Continually Merciful (Bismillah ar-Rahman ar-Rahim)*, encouraging us to recognize how we and all of creation are held within the womb of God's nurturing Love.

It is acknowledged through the Qur'an that for our benefit, messenger upon messenger has been sent to us, community by community. *Ayats* ("Signs") arrive forming into words and intentions in the hearts of the servants of Divine Reality, hearts receptive to the overflowing fountain of guidance pouring from our Infinite Source, from *Haqq* (that which is Truly Real).[4] We are reminded

---

[4] See, for instance, *Surah al-An'am* 6:73:

And He/She it is who has created the heavens and the earth in accordance with an inner Truth [Haqq]—*and the Day He/She says, "Be," it is. His word is the Truth.*

And *Surah Al-'Imran* 3:3–7:

Step by step it is He/She who has sent down to you this Book, within

that everything is created with Truth (*bil Haqq*), yet we as human beings are given the capacity to choose to align with *Haqq* or to turn away.

There need be no strife among us; Divine Reality invites us to Unity—to *the abode of Peace.*[5] He/She invites us to *run the race for the good and beautiful*[6] no matter what our individual faith. In the Qur'an it is recognized that we have been created in diverse communities, *that we might come to know each other.*[7] We can come to see that each human being has been given different gifts, bestowals of the Qualities shining from Divine Reality for each of us to discover and share, and from which to learn. We are reminded in the Qur'an that God could have created us all as one—He/She could have *rooted the human being in one place*[8] that we might have no chance to stray. Instead, Divine Reality gave us our freedom so that we might turn to It with open heart, that we might know the joy of Love blossoming and coming to fruition and experience the

---

Truth [bil Haqq], *confirming what remains of earlier Revelation; for it is He/She who bestowed the Torah and the Gospel,*

before, as a guidance to humankind—it is He/She who has sent down the criterion for discerning right from wrong. Witness how grievous suffering comes to those who are bent on denying God's Signs—for Divine Reality is Almighty, the Rectifier of Wrongs.

Truly, nothing on earth or in the heavens is hidden from God.

It is He/She who forms and prepares you in the wombs as He/She wills. There is no Reality but He/She, the Almighty, the Truly Wise.

It is He/She who has sent down to you from on high this Book. Within it are signs [ayat *(verses)*] *firmly rooted—these are the "Mother of the Book"* [Umm al-Kitab *(the life-giving and nourishing essence of the Revelation)*].

[5] Qur'an, *Surah Yunus* 10:25.
[6] Qur'an, *Surah al-Maida* 5:48.
[7] Qur'an, *Surah al-Hujurat* 49:13.
[8] Qur'an, *Surah Ya Sin* 36:67.

whole range of feeling and knowing, discovering within ourselves the abundance of certainty.

Within the Islamic tradition, it is expressed that even the angels were not strong enough to bear this challenge; only the heart of the human being has such capacity to open fully to the vastness that is "God," to encompass all the Names.[9] Rather than a microcosm, the human being is the macrocosm. As Mevlana Jalaluddin Rumi has said, "You are a dewdrop that contains the entire sea." What was revealed to the Prophets and deeply understood by the wise might be revealed to our own hearts and minds if we would open to their words and truly listen. And *God is the Light of the heavens and the earth*[10] and it is God *who leads us out of the depths of darkness into the Light*[11] and who has given the Qur'an as *a clear light*[12] and *a mercy*[13] to all the worlds, to all levels of being.

Say: "We have faith in Divine Reality,
and in what has been revealed to us,
and what was revealed to Abraham,
Isma'il, Isaac, Jacob, and the Tribes,
and in that given to Moses, Jesus,
and all the prophets from their Sustainer and Cherisher,
and we make no distinction between them,
and to God we bow in surrender."

[Qur'an, *Surah Al-'Imran* 3:84]

---

[9] See *Ninety-Nine Names of the Beloved: Intimations of the Beauty and Power of the Divine,* Camille Hamilton Adams Helminski, Sweet Lady Press, 2017.

[10] Qur'an, *Surah an-Nur* 24:35.

[11] Qur'an, *Surah al-Ahzab* 33:43.

[12] Qur'an, *Surah an-Nisa* 4:174.

[13] Qur'an, *Surah al-'Araf* 7:204.

The Prophets all saw by the light of the same Sun and spoke with the voice of the same Heart. It was surely this overflowing Love that was received by Beloved Maryam in the sanctuary, that Love in which she most deeply trusted. It was she who taught Zachariah the vastness of this Love as in her presence he witnessed the overflowing abundance of Divine sustenance; she told him, *"See how God provides for whom He/She wills, beyond all reckoning."*[14] Zachariah, himself, there in the sanctuary was then moved to pray to God for pure offspring.[15] May we each keep the flow going through God's abundant grace. Continually we are reminded and instructed to share of the blessings that come to us:

You will never attain true Goodness [al-birra, al-Barr]
unless you bestow on others of what you yourselves truly love;
and whatever you spend, certainly, God knows.

[Qur'an, *Surah Al-'Imran* 3:92]

And surely, the more we participate in that flow, the more intimacy with the Beloved is granted, and that which is *within the Presence of God is the most beautiful.*[16] With the knowledge flowing from His/Her Presence, we are enabled to stand in Truth, witnessing to the Majesty of the Infinite Grace of our Loving Sustainer

---

[14] Qur'an, *Surah Al-'Imran* 3:37.

[15] See *The Way of Mary: Maryam, Beloved of God*, by Camille Hamilton Adams Helminski, Sweet Lady Press, 2021, chapters I and II.

[16] Qur'an, *Surah Al-'Imran* 3:195:
   Truly, I will put right their wrongs, and admit them to gardens beneath which rivers flow—a recompense from the Presence of God, and from His/Her Presence is the most beautiful of recompense.

and turning to serve His/Her creation as a true *khalifa*, representative of God, guardian of the Trust of Being, bringing others into that Radiance, sharing love, and the fruition of Love, God willing. Of course, we will be challenged,[17] but always, the Friend and Guide *is with us, wherever we may be.*[18] The Qur'an is a voice for wholeness, for unity, encouraging harmony within the human being and among human beings and the whole of our environment, all of creation. In the Qur'an it is said: *The only religion with God is self-surrender.*[19] When all our actions are in consonance with the Divine Order and Will, we are surrendered to that Truth that is at the core of all that exists. Even as Beloved Maryam completely surrendered, in full trust, to the unfolding of what was to come, which she alone would bear. Surely, Prophet Muhammad, also, took much inspiration from her example; within the Qur'an she is spoken of with great honor, as the highest example of the purely receptive soul. This surrender of the self is, essentially, what *Islam* means—surrender to what Is, knowing we could not design a better portion than the One who created us and seeks the best for us, even more than we are seeking Him/Her—the Source of All Subsistence. We have been given will to accompany the unfolding with the best effort, eyes to discern the best way to proceed, hearts to know by longing, and ears to hear the Words of guidance that have been given through all

---

[17] Qur'an, *Surah Al-'Imran* 3:142:

Do you think you could enter the Garden without Divine Reality knowing how you have striven to your utmost and knowing how you are patient in adversity?

[18] Qur'an, *Surah al-Hadid* 57:4.

[19] Qur'an, *Surah Al-'Imran* 3:19.

manner of beings—the angels, the bees, the roar of the lion, and the song of the Nightingales of God, calling us to let go of the baggage weighing us down—the encumbrances of the wayward, resistant ego. So many have shown us that it is this surrender into the arms of the Beloved that opens the door for *Salaam* (the Peace of God) to pour through, that we might be recreated by Love.

Within the Qur'an, there is an immense beauty, an immense Compassion, a sense of heart which could be of nourishment to many in the English-speaking world who may not have yet come to know the Qur'an but who also find themselves thirsting in a "desert," even as Muhammad was thirsting before the coming of Revelation. Within the Qur'an there is also a stringency revealed; we are cautioned to be mindful—one must bear the consequences of one's actions; this is simply the law of nature, the law of "karma," but as the Qur'an proclaims over and over again, at the commencement of each *surah*, *"Bismillah ar-Rahman ar-Rahim"*: *In the Name of God, the Infinitely Compassionate and Infinitely Merciful*; this message is coming to us from the Compassionate womb of Creation. Everything is held within the Compassion of our Source, and whatever stringency is manifested, it is always overwhelmed by and held within this Infinite Compassion.[20] So much needs rebalancing in our world. Yet we are reminded by the Qur'an that always, the Infinite Mercy of Forgiveness, the possibility of realignment with our Source, is waiting. *Subhanallah, Ya Rabb al-'Alameen!* Glory be to God! O Sustainer and Educator, Cherisher of All Worlds!

---

[20] Qur'an, *Surah al-A'raf* 7:156.

This translation has been much informed by the work of Muhammad Asad and Yusuf Ali, for whose enlightening labors we are so deeply grateful, and the open-hearted sharings of the mystic Mevlana Jalaluddin Rumi and his mentor Shams of Tabriz, and a long lineage of saints and teachers following the inspiration of Prophet Muhammad, he who recognized all the prophets before him in a long lineage of transmission of the Divine Message. Wishing not to encumber the Message, we have refrained from appending footnotes to the translation of the text. We have included just a few parenthetical openings of meaning of the Arabic, interspersed, and the transliteration of a few key passages or terms to keep them more at the fore of remembrance. The transliterations we have rendered in a simplified form to, God willing, be less cumbersome for English speakers. Translation is always a challenge—to keep intact the meaning and yet convey from one language to another. The original word "translation" arose as an expression of the action of conveying the bones of a saint from one place to another . . . a holy endeavor. We pray that this offering might be of support to hearts, as each opens to hear the enlivening Message of Love from our Ever-Loving, Enlivening Source. May that Most Beautiful and Most Gracious One forgive our mistakes and errors and make fruitful this offering that comes to you, dear reader, as together we witness the communication of that Greatest Love that encompasses and supports us every day and night of our lives, even when we fail to recognize It. The Qur'an calls to us to open our eyes and our hearts, so we might witness that

Wherever you turn, there is the Face of God.[21] For truly all
around us *there are signs to see for those who reflect.*[22] May the
Light of the words of the Qur'an strengthen us in that
which is right and enable us to live justly on this earth,
without spreading corruption and with tenderness.

Surely there is so much that needs rectifying in
our human inhabited world; may we strive for Truth,
learning to let go of our resentments and attachments,
opening our hearts to each other in compassion,
compassion gifted to us through our Infinitely Compassionate Source. May we remember that "Time began in
a Garden,"[23] and to the Garden we may return —with
God's gracious assistance and our own renewed intentions, and the polishing of our hearts and actions, so
that we might be people who do *the good and beautiful* and
the whole blessing of the Garden, trees giving shade and
fruit and waters of blessing, might be with us.[24] May we

---

[21] Qur'an, *Surah al-Baqarah* 2:115.

[22] Qur'an, *Surah al-Jathiyah* 45:13.

[23] Saying based upon Bible, Genesis 2:8.

And the Lord God planted a garden eastward in Eden; and there he put the man whom he had formed.

And see, also, Qur'an:

O Adam, dwell, you and your wife, in this garden. [Qur'an, *Surah al-A'raf* 7:19]

O humankind, be conscious of your Sustainer, who created you all out of a single soul, and out of it brought forth its mate, and out of the two spread forth multitudes of men and women. And be ever conscious of God—through whom you ask of each other—and reverence the wombs that bore you. Truly, God is Ever-watching over you. [Qur'an, *Surah an-Nisa* 4:1]

[24] Qur'an, *Surah al-Baqarah*:

Give glad tidings to those who have faith and do the deeds of wholeness and reconciliation that for them are gardens beneath which rivers flow. [Qur'an, *Surah al-Baqarah* 2:25] keep our alignment with the Wholeness, as Shams of Tabriz reminds us:

> Those who catch hold of a branch, will break it and fall, but those who take hold of the trunk of the tree will gain all the branches. They are content with the abode of the Beloved . . . . Now, there is a hidden meaning in these words—it is a clear example of *None but God and the firmly-rooted know its meaning.*[25]

When firmly-rooted, aligned with Divine Reality, a heart can open, and insights are revealed. Within Truth, layer upon layer of meaning opens—many say seven levels of meaning unfold[26]—indicating the intimate levels of

---

[25] *Rumi's Sun: The Teachings of Shams of Tabriz*, translated by Refik Algan and Camille Adams Helminski, Threshold Books, 2020: "*Be of the Firmly-rooted,*" p.284–285. See *Surah Al-'Imran* 3:7–8:

None know its ultimate, complete meaning but God. And so, those who are deeply-rooted in knowledge say: "We have faith in it—the whole of it is from our Sustainer; though none grasp the remembrance except those of tender heart and discerning insight.

"O our Sustainer! Do not let our hearts swerve from the Truth, after You have guided us, and from Your Presence, gift us with compassion. Truly, You are the Giver of Gifts!

[26] Within Islamic mysticism seven stages of the soul are recognized: *nafs al-ammarah*—the commanding self (commanding to follow its desires), *nafs al-lawammah*—the repentant self (the self that repents of its waywardness), *nafs al-mulhamah*—the inspired self (the stage of the self when one recognizes more fully one's connection with the Divine Reality), *nafs al-mutmainnah*—the contented or tranquil self (the one who begins to be content with God's Presence); *nafs ar-radiyah*—the pleased self (the one who is pleased with all that God gives); *nafs al-mardiyah*—the self that has become pleasing (to God); *nafs as-safiyyah*—the purified self.

meaning possible when a heart is deeply listening, looking within the realms of Truth through which we are ever created anew. Again, as Shams of Tabriz reminds us:

> The hearts of the people of God are very wide and open. They are as boundless and limitless as the heavens. All of these heavens turn under such a one's heart.
>
> There is good news in the holy tradition (*hadith qudsi*),[27] "I have prepared such a thing for My good servants that no eye has seen, and no ear has heard, nor has it been revealed to the heart of any human being."[28]

The Islamic mystic, Mevlana Jalaluddin Rumi, continually reminds us of the healing and vivifying radiance

---

As Shams of Tabriz instructs, "No other sight can kill the cluster of the desires of the commanding self, *nafs al-ammarah*, as well as its witnessing of the beauty within the universe of the heart. When it sees the universe of God's beauty, it immediately weakens." (Refer to *Rumi's Sun, op cit.*, p. 136.) And so, little by little, we may arrive at higher stations of the soul and through God's grace see with new eyes, until more and more firmly rooted within the Presence of Divine Reality, we may be gifted with seeing purely, comprehending with the Light of God.

[27] *Hadith Qudsi*: A communication from the Divine, conveyed through the heart of the Prophet Muhammad, beyond the frame of the Qur'an.

[28] *Rumi's Sun, op.cit.*, p. 286.

Shams also reminds us of the *hadith* of Prophet Muhammad, from his own heart: "The *hadith* 'I have such a moment with God that neither a prophet with a book nor an angel close to God can enter in between us' is an invitation, not just a state. This means, 'Do something like this, so that this state may also be yours.'" (See *Rumi's Sun*, p. 128.)

of Love, and of the Kernel of kernels, *Lubb al-lubab*, the "Secret of secrets," hidden deep within the heart of Reality.

How many a generous rain has poured,
so that the sea could scatter pearls!
How many a Sun of Blessing has shone,
so that clouds and seas might learn generosity!

The Sunbeams of Wisdom struck the soil,
so that earth might receive seed:
the soil is faithful to its trust—
whatever you sow, you reap.

The soil's faithfulness comes from that Faithful One,
since the Sun of Justice shines on it.
Until springtime brings the touch of God,
the earth doesn't reveal her secrets.

[Rumi, *Mathnawi* I: 506–511]

Rumi and Shams of Tabriz remind us that the Qur'an is "a shy bride," that we must look with eyes of love to witness her true beauty, that she, herself, might feel secure in revealing it to us. As the completion counsel of *Surah Al-'Imran* calls to us, in encouragement for this journey into Wholeness:

O you who have come to faith! Persevere in patience,
and keep striving with one another in patience,
and keep your connection, and remain conscious of Divine Reality,
so that you might truly attain felicity.
[Ya ayyuha al-lazheena amanu, asbiru, wa saabiru, wa raabitu,
wattaqu Allaha, laallakum tuflihuun.]

[Qur'an, *Surah Al-'Imran* 3:200]

Al-Fatiha

(The Opening)

Bismillah ar-Rahman ar-Rahim

With the Name of God, the Infinitely Compassionate and Continually Merciful—

Praise is God's, Sustainer and Cherisher of all worlds—

the Infinitely Compassionate and Continually Merciful,

Sovereign of the Day of Recognition—

You alone do we worship and serve; You alone do we ask for help.

Guide us on the clear path,

the path of those who have received Your blessing; not the path of those who have brought stringency upon themselves, nor of those who wander into confusion.

Al-Baqarah

(The Cow)

In the Name of God, the Infinitely Compassionate,
the Continually Merciful
[*Bismillah ar-Rahman ar-Rahim*]

Alif. Lam. Mim.

This book, let there be no doubt, is a guidance for all
the God-conscious,

those who trust in the Unseeable-Unnamed, who
are rooted steadfastly in prayer, and who open-heartedly
bestow from the sustenance We have provided for them,

and who trust in that which has been sent down
to you, and that which was sent down before you, and
who have reached certainty through nearness with the
Hereafter—

they are following guidance from their Sustainer; it is
they who attain felicity.

As for those who turn away in denial, it is the same
to them whether you counsel them or you don't; they will
not have faith.

God has covered over their hearts and the possibility
of their turning, and their hearing, and veiled their sight;
mighty is their chastisement.

Among the people there are those who say, "We trust
in God and in the 'Day' of the Hereafter, but they do not
really trust;

3

they would proudly deceive God and those who have faith, but they only deceive themselves and do not see it,

because in their hearts is disease, and God (the Unity of all existence) increases their disease; their torment is grievous, because they are cut off by their deception.

When it is said to them, "Do not spread corruption on this good earth!" they say, "We only want to do good deeds."

Indeed, it is they who spread corruption, but they do not see it.

When it is said to them, "Trust as the others trust," they say, "Should we trust like fools trust?" No, surely, they are the fools; but they are unaware.

When they come face to face with those who trust, they say, "We trust," but when they are alone with those who have turned away in denial, they say, "We are with you; we were mocking them."

The Unity of God will render them ridiculous and extend the rope of their transgressions, so that they will wander further in their blindness.

These are those who have traded guidance for perplexity; their trade is without benefit. They have lost their way.

Their likeness is that of someone who has kindled a fire—when it lit up all around them, God took away their light and left them in obscurity, such that they cannot perceive.

Deaf, unable to speak, blind, they could not turn back to find the way.

Another likeness is that of a cloud heavy with rain from the heavens—within it are darkness and thunder and lightning—they put their fingers in their ears to keep out the crash of the thunder, stunned with fear of dying,

4

yet God encompasses the deniers (those who attempt to conceal the Truth).

The lightning seizes their perception; when the light shines, they walk within it; when the darkness increases, they are stilled. If God willed, He/She could take away their capacity to hear and to see, for God has power over all things.

O humankind! Worship and serve your Sustainer, who created you and those who came before you, so that you may learn to be conscious of God,

who has made the earth a resting-place for you, and the sky your canopy, and sent down rain from the heavens and so brought forth fruits for your sustenance; then don't claim that there is any power that could rival God, when you know.

And if you are in doubt as to that which We have sent down to Our servant, then produce a *surah* like it, and call your own witnesses besides Allah if your purpose is sincere.

But if you cannot—and surely you cannot—then fear the fire that burns humans (by their own kindling of it), and even hardened stones, that is prescribed for those in denial.

But give glad tidings to those who have faith and do the deeds of wholeness and reconciliation that for them are gardens beneath which rivers flow. Whenever they are nourished with its fruits they say, "Why, it is this with which we were fed beforehand," for they are given corresponding gifts; and they have there pure partners, and there they abide forever.

Truly, God does not disdain using metaphors, for the lowly or the exalted. Those who have faith know it is Truth from their Sustainer. But those who are in denial say, "What does God intend by this metaphor?" Through it He causes many to wander in confusion and many He guides to the clear path; but He does not cause any to lose their way except those who have already fallen into transgression.

Those who break the bond with God after it has been pledged, and who break apart what God has enjoined to be held together, and spread corruption upon good, fruitful land—it is they who are in loss, themselves.

How can you turn your back on God in denial, seeing that you were without life and He gave you life? Then He will cause you to die, and will bring you to flourishing life again, and again to Him you will return.

It is He who has created for you all things on earth, and He brought together His design, arranging in proportion the seven heavens, and of all things He is the Knower.

Behold, your Sustainer said to the angels, "I will create a representative caretaker on earth." They said, "Will you place there one who will spread corruption and shed blood; while we praise You and glorify Your Purity?" He said, "Truly, I know what you know not."

And He taught Adam all the Names; then He displayed all before the angels and said, "Tell Me the names of these if you speak the truth."

They said, "Glory be to You, we have no knowledge except that which You have taught us: it is You who are the All-Knowing, the Most Wise."

He said, "O Adam! Tell them their names." When he had told them, God said, "Didn't I tell you that I know the hidden reality of heaven and earth, and I know what you reveal and what you conceal."

And We said to the angels, "Bow down to Adam," and they bowed down. Except for Iblis—he refused, full of pride—he was in the state of the deniers (who turn away from Truth).

We said, "O Adam! Dwell in tranquility, you and your partner, in the Garden; and eat of the abundance as you will, but do not approach this tree (of separation), or you will find yourself in a state of darkness."

Then Satan (who provokes separation) made them stumble, forsaking that state of felicity in which they had been abiding. We said, "Descend, you with discord between yourselves; on earth will be your dwelling and where you will find your footing and provisions for a while."

Then the human beings learned words of inspiration from their Sustainer—their Sustainer turned towards them, for He/She is Ever-Accepting of Repentance, the Continually Merciful [*at-Tawwab, ar-Rahim*].

We said, "All of you descend from here; and if, as is sure, there comes to you guidance from Me, whoever follows My guidance, they shall not fear, nor shall they grieve.

But those who turn away in denial and reject Our Signs, they shall be companions of the fire—abiding within it.

O children of Israel! Deeply remember the blessings I have bestowed upon you, and fulfill your covenant with Me as I fulfill My covenant with you, and do not be in awe of anyone or anything but Me.

And trust in what I send down, confirming the truth of that which is already with you, and do not be the foremost among those who turn away from its truth; do not exchange My Communications for a pittance. Of Me be conscious.

And do not cover over truth with falsehood, and do not hide the truth when you know;

and be steadfast in prayer, and in charity, and bow in prayer with all those who are humble.

Do you enjoin other people to be righteous and honest and forget to be so yourselves? And yet you meditate upon the Scriptures—will you not try to understand?

Seek help in steadfast patience and prayer; it is a great challenge for all but those who approach in humility,

those who know with certainty that they will meet their Sustainer and Cherisher, and that to Him/Her they will return.

O descendants of Israel (of "he who struggles with God"), deeply remember the blessings with which I gifted you, above all creatures.

And be conscious of a day when no soul shall avail another, nor shall intercession be accepted, nor ransom, nor succor arrive.

And remember when We delivered you from Pharaoh's people, who afflicted you with cruelty, slaughtering your sons and only letting your women live—a mighty trial from your Sustainer!

And remember We split the sea for you, saving you, and caused Pharaoh's people to drown before your eyes.

And remember when We apportioned for Moses forty nights, and, while he was absent, you turned towards the calf, erring in darkness.

Yet, even after that, We erased your sin with forgiveness, that you might be grateful.

And remember We gave Moses the Scripture—the Criterion of discernment—so that you might be guided rightly.

And remember Moses said to his people, "O my people! You have wronged your own selves by worshipping the calf, so turn towards your Maker, let your egos die (coming to know your real self); that would be better for you in the sight of the One who made you. And thereupon He/She turned towards you, for He/She is Ever-Turning Towards those in repentance, Continually Merciful.

And remember when you said, "O Moses, truly we will not trust in you until we see God clearly apparent!" Whereupon mighty thunder and lightning stunned you, as you looked,

but We raised you up again after you had been as though dead, so that you might be grateful.

And We covered you with clouds to comfort you with shade, and sent down to you manna of bounty and quail of consolation: "Partake of the wholesome things We provide for you as sustenance." And they did no harm to Us, but only themselves did they wrong.

And remember We said, "Enter this land, and eat of its abundant provision as you will, but enter the gate humbly, and say, 'Remove from us the burden of our sin,' and We shall forgive you your errors and magnify those who do that which is good and beautiful."

But the wrong-doers corrupted the words We had sent down, and so We sent down calamity from the heavens upon those wrong-doers, because of their erring ways.

And remember, Moses prayed for water for his people; We said, "Strike the rock with your staff"—and twelve springs gushed forth from within it. Each tribe knew its own place for water. So eat and drink of the sustenance provided by God, and do not act wrongly by spreading corruption on this good earth.

And remember when you said, "O Moses, we can't keep eating just one kind of food; pray to your Lord for us that He might bring forth from the earth its produce—its herbs and its cucumbers, its garlic, its lentils, and onions." He said, "Will you trade that which is better for that which is less? Return then in shame to Egypt, and then you can have that which you are wanting." And so they covered themselves with shame and misery; they drew towards themselves the stringency of Divine Reality, because they continually rejected the Communications of God and slayed His Messengers, without reason; they kept opposing God and acting unjustly.

Truly, those who have faith, and those who follow the Jewish faith, and the Christians, and the Sabians—all who have faith in Divine Reality and the Day of the Hereafter and do the deeds of wholeness and reconciliation—shall have their recompense with their Sustainer; they shall have no fear, neither shall they grieve.

And witness! We accepted your firm covenant, and raised high above you the Mountain of Sinai: "Hold fast with all your strength to that which We have given you, and deeply remember it; that you might be steadfast in consciousness of God."

But then you turned away; had it not been for the bountiful favors of God and His/Her tender mercy to you, you would surely have been among the lost.

For you knew well those among you who turned aside from the sacredness of the Sabbath, and We said to them, "Be ashamed in confusion (as those of false pretense)!"

And We made them an example for their time and for all those who come after, and a warning for those who would be vigilant in God-consciousness.

And witness, Moses said to his people, "Behold, God commands you to sacrifice a cow." They said, "Do you take us for fools?" He said, "I seek refuge in God from such ignorant foolishness."

They said, "Pray to your Lord for us, to make clear what it is." He answered, "He indicates that the cow shall be neither too old nor too young, of a useful, middle age. Now do that which you are commanded."

They said, "Pray on our behalf to your Sustainer to ask what color." Moses answered, "Behold, He says it is to be a golden yellow cow, bright of hue, pleasing to the beholder."

They said, "Ask on our behalf for your Sustainer to make clear to us what exactly she is, for to us all cows are similar. If God wills, we might then be guided."

Moses answered, "He says it is to be a cow neither trained to plow the earth nor to water crops, sound without blemish." They said, "At last you have brought the whole truth." Then they offered her in sacrifice, though they were almost incapable of doing it.

Because you had slain a soul and then blamed each other—although God will always reveal whatever you conceal—

We said, "Strike that with part of it." And so, God brings the dead to life, and shows His Signs to you, so that you might understand.

And yet, even after this your hearts were hardened and became like rocks, or even harder, for among rocks there are some from which rivers gush forth, and others that when struck crack open so that from them water pours forth; and there are some that fall down in awe of God. And God is not unmindful of what you do.

Can you then hope that they will put their trust in you?

Seeing that some of them have heard the Word of God and yet corrupted it knowingly, even after having understood it?

And see, how when these meet people of faith, they say, "We have faith," but when they come together, privately, they say to each other, "Will you divulge to them what God has disclosed to you, allowing them to use it in argument against you, before your Lord?" Won't you understand?

Don't they know that God knows what they keep secret and what they reveal?

And there are among them those who are illiterate, who do not know the Book, but only their wishful desires, and their conjectures.

Then woe to those who write the Book from their own hands, and then claim, "This is from God," in order to acquire some gain. Woe to them for what their hands have written! And woe to them for whatever they may have gained!

And they say, "The fire won't touch us but for a few days." Say, "Have you taken a promise from God—for He never breaks His promise—or do you say about God what you do not know?"

No—those who seek to earn through wrong-doing, and are encircled by their sins—they are companions of the fire, and there abide.

Whereas those who have faith and do the deeds of wholeness and reconciliation, they are companions of the garden—there do they abide.

And behold, We accepted this covenant from the children of Israel: to worship none but God, to act beautifully towards your parents, your relatives, the orphans, and the helpless; to speak beautifully with the people; to establish steadfast prayer and offer the charity that purifies. And yet, except for a few of you, you turned away; and still you disregard it.

And behold, We accepted your covenant to shed no blood among you, nor to drive anyone among you from your homes, and this you solemnly agreed; you can bear witness to it.

And yet, even after this, it is you who slay one another, and drive some among you from their homes, helping one another in wrong-doing against them, out of spite. And if they come to you as captives, you ransom them, though you had no right to send them away. So is it only part of the Book in which you have faith, and you turn away from the rest? But what is the recompense of those among you who behave like this, except disgrace in this world, and on the Day of Standing, a mighty chastisement? For God is not unmindful of what you do.

Those are the ones who purchase the life of this world with the Hereafter—but this will not lighten their torment, nor shall they be helped.

For truly, We entrusted unto Moses the Divine Scripture, and caused Messenger after Messenger to follow him; We gave Jesus, the son of Mary, clear Signs and strengthened him with the Holy Spirit. Yet whenever a Messenger comes to you, with what you may not like, are you not proudly insolent? Some of them you have denied, and others you kill!

They proclaim, "Our hearts are already full of knowledge!" No, but God has turned away from them because they have turned away. Little faith do they have.

Whenever there comes to them a Scripture from God, confirming what is with them—even though long ago they had prayed for victory over those who deny

13

the Truth—when there comes to them that which they should recognize, they deny it. But God's denial is the recompense of those who are in denial.

Miserable is the price for which they have bartered their souls, for they deny what God has sent down, in proud envy that God should send down His Grace to any of His servants, as pleases Him. And thus have they brought upon themselves intense stringency upon stringency; a shameful suffering comes to those who cover over the Truth.

For when they are told, "Trust in what God has sent down," they say, "We have faith in what was sent down to us"; yet they reject anything else, even if it is Truth confirming what is with them. Say, "Why, then, have you killed the prophets of God who came before, if you were people of faith?"

And there came to you Moses, with clear Signs; and then, in his absence, you worshipped the calf, and acted wrongfully.

And remember We accepted your covenant, and We raised the Mountain of Sinai high above you: "Hold firmly to what We have entrusted to you, and pay attention to it." They say, "We have heard, but we disobey"—for their hearts are filled with love of the calf, because of their ungrateful denial. Say: "Calamitous are the commands of your faith—if such a state is any kind of faith."

Say: "If the Abode of the Hereafter is especially for you with God, and not for anyone else, you should long for death, if you are sincere."

But they will never seek it, because of what their hands have wrought that goes before them; and God knows full well the wrong-doers.

And you will indeed find them, of all people, most covetous of life, even more than idolators; each one wishes he could live a thousand years, even though such a long life could not distance torment from him—for God sees well all that they do.

Say: "Whoever fights against Gabriel (the angel who restores wholeness to that which has been broken)"—for he brings down the revelation to your heart by God's will, a confirmation of that which came before, and guidance and glad tidings for those who have faith—

"whoever opposes Divine Reality and Its angels and messengers, including Gabriel and Michael—truly, the Divine Reality opposes those who ungratefully deny the Truth."

For clear messages have We sent down to you; and none turn away but those who are willfully perverse.

Isn't it so that every time they make a covenant some of them throw it away? No, truly, many of them are faithless.

And when there has come to them a messenger from Divine Reality, confirming what was with them, some of those who received the Book before threw the Scripture of God away, behind their backs, as though they were unaware,

and they have followed what the wicked ones used to practice who challenged Solomon's power—for it was not Solomon, but the wicked who taught people magic and such things as came down at Babylon through the two (fallen) angels, Harut and Marut—although these two never taught anyone anything without first declaring, "We are but a temptation to wickedness; do not deny the Truth!" And they learned from them the means to sow discord between spouses. But they could not so harm anyone except as God might allow, and so they acquired a knowledge that was of harm to themselves, rather than what could have been of benefit, even though they knew that those who purchased it would have no share of the happiness of the Hereafter. And miserable was the price for which they sold their own souls—had they but known it!

And had they kept their trust and been vigilant in consciousness, how much better would have been the recompense from their Sustainer—had they but known it!

O you who have attained to faith, do not say disrespectfully (to the Messenger), "Listen to us," but rather say, "Be patient with us," and listen (yourselves), for grievous torment awaits those who deny the Truth.

Neither those who deny the Truth from among those of the Book nor the polytheists would like to see any goodness from your Sustainer bestowed upon you. But God will choose for His special Mercy whomever He will—for God is Gloriously Magnificent in the bestowal of favored blessing.

None of Our Communications do We abrogate or consign to oblivion without replacing it with something better or similar. Don't you know that God has Power over all things?

Don't you know that to God belongs the dominion of the heavens and the earth? And other than Divine Reality you have no protector or help?

Would you question the Messenger as before Moses was questioned? Whoever chooses to turn from trust to denial has already strayed from the sound path.

Out of selfish envy, many of the followers of earlier revelation would like to turn you back from faith to denial, even after the Truth has become manifest to them; but forgive and forbear until God shall accomplish His purpose. For God has Power over all things.

And be steadfast in prayer and constant in purifying charity. And whatever good you send forth for your souls, you shall find it with God. For God sees well all that you do.

And they claim, "None shall enter the Garden unless he be a Jew," or "a Christian." Those are their wishful beliefs. Say, "Produce your proof, if what you say is true."

Surely no; whoever surrenders his or her whole self to Divine Reality in a beautiful way, he or she will receive recompense from his or her Sustainer—all such need have no fear, neither shall they grieve.

The Jews say, "The Christians have no valid ground to stand upon"; and the Christians say, "The Jews have no valid ground to stand upon." Yet they both follow the Book. Those who were without knowledge have said the same thing as they say. But it is God who will judge between them on the Day of Standing, with regard to all that about which they disagree.

And who could be more unjust than one who forbids the remembrance of God's Name in any of the houses of worship of God, one who even strives to ruin them? They should not even enter them except in awe. For them there is nothing but disgrace in this world, and in the Hereafter mightily grievous suffering.

To God belong the East and the West, and wherever you turn, there is the Face of God. Behold, God is Infinite, All-Encompassing, All-Knowing. [*Wa lillahi al-mashriqu waal-maghribu fa-aynama tuwallu fathamma wajhu Allahi, inna Allahu Wasi'un 'Alim.*]

17

They say, "God has taken unto Himself a son." Glory be to God, subtle beyond all—no, to Him/Her belongs all that is in the heavens and on earth: everything is in humble, devoted service to Him/Her.

He/She is the Originator of the heavens and the earth; and when He/She wills a thing to be, He/She but says to it, "Be!"—and it is.

And those without knowledge say, "Why doesn't Divine Reality speak to us, or show a Sign to us?" Even so, those before them spoke similar words—their hearts are alike. Indeed, We have made clear the Signs to people of inner certainty, those who are steadfast in nearness.

Truly, We have sent you as a Messenger with joyful tidings of the Truly Real and with cautions. And you shall not be held accountable for the companions of the burning fire (of desire and covetousness).

For never will the Jews be pleased with you, nor the Christians, unless you follow their dictates of religion. Say, "God's guidance is the only guidance." And truly if you were to follow their wishes after the knowledge that has come to you, you would have none to protect you from God, none to bring you support.

Those unto whom We have entrusted the Book, and follow it as it ought to be followed, it is they who have faith in it; those who choose to turn away in denial—it is they who are in loss.

O children of Israel! Remember deeply [*zhikr*] the blessings with which I gifted you, and how I favored you above the worlds.

Then be conscious of the Day when one soul shall not be of help to another, nor shall compensation be accepted from anyone, nor shall intercession be of any use, nor shall they be aided.

And remember that Abraham was tried by his Lord with words of commanding power which he fulfilled— He said, "I will make you a leader of the people." And he implored, "And also from my offspring!" He answered, "But My Promise is not reached by those who are oppressors."

And behold! We made the House (*al-Bayt*; the Kaaba, the innermost heart) a place of return and gathering for humankind, and a sanctuary; take then the place where Abraham stood as your place of prayer. And We covenanted with Abraham and Ishmael that they should sanctify My House for all who walk around it, for all who abide there in retreat, and those who bow and prostrate themselves.

And behold, Abraham prayed, "O my Sustainer, make this a land of tranquility, and feed the people with its fruitfulness—those among them who trust in God and the Last Day." He [God] said, "Those who turn away from the Truth and are ungrateful—for a little while will I allow them to enjoy their pleasure, but they will eventually be compelled into the torment of the fire—a terrible journey's end."

And behold Abraham and Ishmael raised up the foundations of the House: "O our Sustainer, accept this from us; for You are the All-Hearing, the All-Knowing [*as-Sami, al-'Alim*]!

"O our Sustainer, make us both surrender ourselves unto You! And make out of our offspring a community who will surrender themselves to you. And show us our ways of worship and turn with mercy toward us, for You are Continually Re-Turning, Accepting of Repentance, Continually Merciful [*at-Tawwab, ar-Rahim*].

"O our Sustainer, raise up from amidst our offspring

19

a Messenger from among themselves who will convey to them Your Signs and convey to them knowledge of the Book and wisdom, and cause them to grow in purity: for You are the Exalted, Most Dear, the All-Wise [*al-'Aziz, al-Hakim*]."

And who would turn away from the Way of Abraham but those who demean their souls with foolishness, since We purified him and raised him high in excellence in this world, and truly, in the Hereafter he will be among those who have done the wholesome good.

When his Sustainer said to him, "Surrender yourself to Me," he said, "I wholeheartedly surrender to the Sustainer and Cherisher of the Worlds."

And this was the legacy Abraham left to his children, and so did Jacob: "O my children! God has granted you a clear, pure Way; then do not die without being surrendered."

No, but you even bear witness that when death came to Jacob, behold, he said to his children, "What will you worship after I am gone?" They answered, "We will worship your God, the God of your forefathers, Abraham, Ishmael, and Isaac—the one Divine Reality, towards which we bow in surrender."

Now those people have passed away. They shall reap the fruit of what they did, and you of what you do. You shall not be asked about what they did.

And they say, "Be a Jew," or "a Christian," "if you would be guided." Say: "No; the Way of Abraham, who turned aside from that which is false, and was not of those who join others with God!"

Say: "We have faith in the Divine Reality, and that which has been bestowed upon us, and that which was sent down to Abraham, Ishmael, Isaac, Jacob, and their

20

descendants, and that which was entrusted to Moses and Jesus, and that which has been entrusted to all the Prophets from their Sustainer: we make no distinction between any of them, and to Him/Her we bow in surrender."

So if they have faith like you have faith, then they are guided; but if they turn away, it is they who have cut themselves off, but God will suffice you, for He/She is All-Hearing, All-Knowing.

(Say, "Our faith is) immersion in God. And who could give a more beautiful hue than God? It is He/She whom we worship and serve."

Say, "Will you argue with us about God, when He/She is our Sustainer as well as your Sustainer? Unto us will be our deeds and unto you yours. It is to Him/Her alone that we are sincerely in service."

"Do you claim that Abraham and Ishmael, and Isaac, and Jacob, and their descendants were 'Jews' or 'Christians'?" Say, "Do you know more than God? And who could be further from the right way than one who conceals evidence bestowed by God? But God is not unmindful of what you do."

Now those people have passed on; their deeds will be accounted to them and unto you what you have earned; and you will not be asked about their deeds.

The foolish among the people will question: "What has turned them away from the orientation of prayer to which they were accustomed?" Say, "To God belongs the East and the West. He/She guides whom He/She wills to a broad straight Way."

And thus have We willed you to be a community of balance, so that you might bear witness to the Truth for humankind, and the Messenger might be a witness to

Truth for you. And We appointed the *qibla* (orientation for prayer), to which you were accustomed, so that those who follow the Messenger might be discerned from those who turn on their heels—it was a great challenge except for those guided by God. And never would God make your faith futile, for God is to all humankind Most Kind, Continually Merciful [*ar-Rauf, ar-Rahim*].

We have seen you often turn your face toward heaven seeking nearness; and now we shall turn you towards a *qibla* through which you will be pleased. Turn then your face toward the Sacred House of Prostration and Prayer: wherever you are turn your face in that direction. People of the Book know well this is the Truth from their Sustainer. And God is not unaware of what you do.

Even if you were to bring all the Signs to the people of the Book, they would not follow your orientation for prayer, nor are you to follow their orientation for prayer, nor do they follow each other's orientation for prayer. And if you were to follow their wishes, after all the knowledge that has come to you, you would indeed be among the wrong-doers.

They to whom We have given the Book know it as they know their own children; but see how some of them conceal the Truth which they know.

The Truth is from your Sustainer. So do not be in doubt.

For each is an orientation toward which his or her face is turned by God, of which He/She is the goal. Strive then to attain the Good. Wherever you may be, God will bring you all together, for God has Power over all things.

From wherever you go forth, turn your face toward the Sacred Place of Prostration [*al-Masjid al-Haram*].

This is indeed the Truth from your Sustainer. And God is not unaware of what you do.

So from wherever you begin, turn your face toward the Sacred Place of Prostration, and wherever you are, turn your face there, that there might be no argument among you and the people, except those who are inclined to act unjustly; fear them not, but be in awe of Me, that I might complete My favors upon you, and you might be guided.

Even so We have sent a Messenger to you from among yourselves, conveying our Messages, and purifying you, and conveying to you knowledge of the scriptures and wisdom, and new knowing.

So remember Me—and I remember you. And give thanks; do not turn away with ingratitude. [*Fa zhkuroonee azhkurkum; Washkuroo lee wala takfuroon.*]

O you who have faith, seek help through steadfast patience and prayer, for God is with those who patiently persevere.

And do not say of those who are killed on God's Way, "They are dead." No, they are alive, but you do not perceive it.

And surely, We shall try you by means of danger, and hunger, and loss of possessions, and lives, and fruitfulness, but give glad tidings to those who patiently persevere—

those who when calamity afflicts them say, "Truly, to God we belong, and truly, to Him/Her we are returning."

It is they upon whom are greetings of blessing from their Sustainer, and tender Mercy, and it is they who are clearly guided.

Behold, As-Safa and Al-Marwah are among the Symbols of God. So if those who come to the House on pilgrimage or a devoted visit lower their wings to encompass them as they walk, no wrong do they do. And if anyone does more good than one is bound to do—surely God is One Who Recognizes Gratitude, All-Knowing.

Behold, if anyone covers over the clear revelation of Signs and the Guidance We have sent down, after We have made it manifest to humankind through the Book— these it is from whom God will turn His/Her blessings far away, and whom all who can judge will reject.

Except for those who experience a turning of heart and make amends, and make known the Truth—it is toward them I turn, for I am the Acceptor of Repentance, Oft Re-Turning, the Continually Merciful.

Behold, as for those who cover over the Truth and die in denial and ingratitude, their portion is the driving away of God's blessing, and that of the angels, and all humankind.

They will persist in that; their suffering will not lighten, nor will respite come to them.

And your God is One God; there is no god but He/ She—the Infinitely Compassionate, the Continually Merciful.

Look around you!—In the creation of the heavens and the earth; in the alternation of night and day; in the sailing of ships through the sea for the benefit of humankind; in the waters which God sends down from the skies, giving life thereby to the earth that was dead; in the creatures of all kinds which He/She spreads there; in the changing of the winds and the clouds that follow them in service, between sky and earth—truly, these are signs for people who reflect.

Yet there are people who still choose to worship others as equal with God—they love them as they should love God. But those who have faith are overflowing in their love of Divine Reality, beyond all else. If only the wrong-doers could see, they would see the terrible suffering incurred—that God is the Creator of all Power, and that Divine Reality is stringent in the bestowal of correction.

Then would those who are followed free themselves of followers—they would see the penalty and cut off all relations with them.

Then those followers would say, "Would that we had a second chance, so we could have cut ourselves off from them as they have cut us off." And so will God show them the result of their deeds as nothing but regrets, nor will there be a way for them out of that fire.

O humankind! Partake of what is lawful on earth and good; and do not follow the path of Satan, the insolent, perverse one, for he is a known enemy of yours;

for he urges you towards what is corrupt and full of shame, and that you should speak of God what you do not know.

When it is said to them, "Follow what God has sent down from on high," some answer, "No, we follow the ways of our forefathers." What? Even if their ancestors were without wisdom or guidance?

The parable of those who turn away in denial is like that of creatures to whom a shepherd cries out, but who hear nothing of the call. Deaf, dumb, and blind, they are empty of understanding.

O you who have faith, partake of the wholesome things that We have provided for you as sustenance, and give thanks to God, if it is He/She you worship and serve.

He/She has prohibited for you only carrion, and blood, and the flesh of swine, and that over which any other name than God's has been invoked; but if one is forced by necessity, without willful waywardness, nor going beyond limits, then he or she is without error, for God is Oft-Forgiving, Continually Merciful.

Truly, those who conceal what God has sent down in the Book, trading it for some miserable gain—they are filling their bellies with fire. God will not speak to them on the Day of Standing, nor purify them; grievous is their chastisement.

It is they who choose error in exchange for guidance and suffering instead of forgiveness—how they persist with the fire!

And so it is; for Divine Reality is sending down the Scriptures with Truth [*bil Haqq*]; indeed, those who argue about it cut themselves off, withdrawing far distant.

True righteousness is not in turning your faces towards the East or the West. Truly righteous is one who trusts in the Divine Reality, in the Day of the Hereafter, and the angels, and Revelation, and the exalted prophets; one who spends of what has been given to one—out of love for Him/Her—upon one's near of kin, and the orphans, and the needy, and the wayfarer, and those who beg, and for the freeing of human beings from slavery; and is steadfast in prayer, and offers purifying charity; they who keep their promises whenever they promise, and are patient in suffering and in difficulty, and in time of danger; it is they who have proved themselves true, and it is they, they who are conscious of God.

O you who have faith! The law of making things equal is prescribed for you in cases of killing—the free (is responsible) as one who is free, one who is a slave as a slave, and the female as a female. If any remission is made by his or her fellow human being, then grant any honorable demand, and make reparations to him or her with handsome gratitude. This is a lightening from your Sustainer and Cherisher, and an act of Mercy. But for the one who willfully goes beyond the bounds of what is right is grievous suffering.

For in the law of just restitution there is life for you, O you of insight—that you might remain conscious of God.

It is prescribed, when death approaches any of you, if he or she is leaving behind any goods, that he or she make a bequest to parents and near of kin according to what is just; this is due from those who are conscious of God.

If anyone intentionally alters the bequest after hearing it, the sin of it shall be upon those who alter it—indeed, God is All-Hearing, All-Knowing.

If, however, anyone fears that the testator has made a mistake or is responsible for a wrong, and brings about a peaceful settlement among the parties, he or she incurs no sin. Truly God is Oft-Forgiving, Continually Merciful.

O you who have attained to faith! Fasting is ordained for you as it was ordained for those before you, so that you might remain conscious of God—

during a certain number of days—but if any of you is ill, or on a journey, the prescribed number may be from later days, and, for those who can, a substitute of feeding one who is in need. But whoever gives more good than he or she is bound to do, is doing good to himself/herself; and if you fast it is goodness for yourselves—if you but knew!

Ramadan is the month in which the Quran was sent down, as a guidance to humankind, clearly evident—for guidance and discernment. And so everyone of you who is present during that month should fast throughout it, but if anyone is ill or on a journey, the prescribed period may be later days. God wills ease for you; He/She does not will difficulty for you, but wants you to complete the prescribed number of days; and glorify Him/Her for He/She has guided you—and perhaps you will be grateful.

And if My servants ask you about Me—truly, I am near. [*Wa-izha sa'alaka 'ibadi 'anni fa-inni qarib.*] I respond to the one who calls Me whenever he or she calls Me; let them then respond to Me, and trust in Me, that they might follow the well-guided way.

Open for you on the night of the fasts is lying with your women. They are as a garment for you and you are as a garment for them. God knows how you were secretly behaving among yourselves, but He turned toward you and erased your error in forgiveness; so now it is open for you to lie with your spouse, and enjoy what God has made lawful for you, and eat and drink (during the nights of the fast) until the white streak of dawn appears distinct from its black; then stay with your fast until the night comes. But do not lie with your spouses during the period you are dwelling in retreat in the mosques. Those are the bounds set by God—so do not approach them. In this way, God makes His signs clear to humankind, that they might remain conscious of Divine Reality.

And do not eat up another's property wrongfully, nor let it fall to legal judgement in order that you might devour wrongfully, knowingly, of abundance that belongs to others.

They ask you about the new moons. Say, "They are indicators of time-frames for humankind, including the pilgrimage." Righteousness does not consist in entering dwellings from behind, but true righteousness is being conscious of God. And so enter dwellings through their appropriate doors, and remain conscious of God, that you might be happy.

And struggle in God's Way against those who struggle against you, but do not transgress unjustly, for God does not love aggressors,

and fight against those wherever you encounter them, and clear them out from where they have cleared you out—for oppression is worse than war. But do not fight against them near the Sacred Place of Prostration, unless they fight you there, but if they do fight you, fight against them, such is the earning of those who consciously conceal the Truth.

But if they cease—witness, God is Oft-Forgiving, Continually Merciful [*al-Ghafur, ar-Rahim*].

And so challenge them until there is no more oppression, and justice and the Way of Divine Reality prevails; but if they cease, all opposition shall cease, except against those who willfully do wrong.

The month that is sacred, as the month that is sacred—and for all that is sacred, there is the law of balance. And if anyone goes beyond your limits, go beyond his or her limits as he or she has gone beyond yours—and be in awe of God, and know that God is with those who are in awe of Him/Her.

And spend in the Way of God, and do not let your own hands throw you into destruction. Do the good and beautiful—truly, God loves the doers of the good and beautiful. [*Wa ahsinu—inna Allaha yuhibbu al-muhsineen.*]

And complete the pilgrimage, and the lesser visit of devotion, in service of Divine Reality. But if you are kept from it, make a gift in sacrifice, as best you may find; and do not cut off the hair from your head until the offering reaches the place of surrender. And if anyone among you is ill or suffering because of his head, in exchange, fast, or give true charity, or offer acts of devotion; and when you are well and secure again, if one wishes to complete the sacred visit or the pilgrimage, he or she may make an offering, as best he or she can find—or if not able, he or she can fast three days during the pilgrimage and seven days upon his or her return, ten days in all, this for those who are not abiding within the Sacred Place of Prostration; and be conscious of God, and know that the Divine Reality is rigorous in responding step by step.

The pilgrimage shall be during the months indicated for it, and whoever engages in the pilgrimage during those shall, while on pilgrimage, refrain from vulgar speech, from all harmful actions, and from arguments; and whatever goodness you may do, God is aware of it. And take provision for the journey, but truly the best provision is God-consciousness—so keep conscious of Me, O you of inner knowing!

Yet you will be doing nothing wrong if you seek to gather some bounty from your Sustainer. And when you flow forth from Arafat (the heights of "Gnosis"), remember [*zhikr*] God at that holy, pure place of perception, and remember Him/Her as the One who guided you after you had lost your way;

and surge onward with all the people who surge onward—and ask God to forgive you your errors, for truly, God is Oft-Forgiving, Continually Merciful.

And when you have completed your rites of devotion, continue to keep God in remembrance [*zhikr*], as you would keep your own parents in remembrance; no, with an even more intensely heartfelt remembrance.

For there are people who pray, "O our Sustainer, give us in this world…"—and such shall have no portion in the Hereafter.

But there are, also, those who pray, "O our Sustainer, grant us goodness in this world and goodness in the Hereafter, and safeguard us from suffering through the fire."

These shall have their nourishment in return for that which they have sought, and God is quick to account.

And remember [*zhikr*] God during the designated days. But if anyone readies to depart in two days, he (or she) shall merit no error, and he or she who stays longer shall merit no error—if he (or she) is conscious of God. And so be conscious of God, and know that unto Him/Her you shall be gathered.

There is a kind of person whose views on the life of this world may please you greatly, and he cites God as witness to what is in his heart, and is most adept in argument.

But whenever he prevails, he spreads corruption on this good earth, causing the destruction of cultivated land and society; and God does not love corruption.

And whenever he is told, "Be conscious of the Divine Reality," his misplaced pride drives him into error, so that the fire suffices him—what a terrible abode.

But there is also a kind of person who would give up his own self, seeking harmonious alignment with Divine Reality; and God is Infinitely Kind and Tender toward His servants.

O you of faith, enter wholeheartedly into the peace of surrender; and do not follow the footsteps of one who is arrogant and corrupt [*shaytan*], for he is clearly your enemy.

And if you should stumble in error after clear signs have come to you, know that God is Almighty, the All-Wise Restorer of Soundness.

Are these people waiting for God to come upon them in the shading clouds, together with the angels—even though by then all will have already been decided? To God all authority returns.

Ask the descendants of Israel how many a clear message We have given them—and if anyone alters God's beneficence, turning away after it has reached him or her, truly, the Divine Reality is stringent in response.

To those who turn away from the Truth in denial, the life of this world is alluring, and so they mock those who trust in the Divine Reality, but those who are conscious of the Divine Reality will be far beyond them on the Day of Standing (and Rebirth). For God bestows sustenance upon whom He/She wills, beyond all reckoning.

All humankind were once one single community, (but when they differed) God uplifted the prophets as bringers of glad tidings and as warners and through them bestowed Revelation from on high, conveying the Truth—so that it might decide between people regarding all about which they had come to differ. Yet the people who had received Revelation, after clear signs had come to them, out of mutual jealousy came to differ among themselves about the Truth. But God guided the faithful to the Truth about which they had differed, for God guides to a clear way the one who wills it.

Do you think you could enter the Garden without enduring such as came to those who went before you? They met with suffering and adversity, and so shaken were they that the Messenger, and the faithful with him, would cry out, "When will God's help come?" O, truly,

God's help is near! [*Ala inna nasra Allahi qareeb.*]

They will ask you as to what they should spend on others. Say, "Whatever of goodness you spend shall be first for your parents, and for close relatives, and for the orphans, and the needy, and the wayfarer; and whatever good you do, truly, God knows well."

Struggle is prescribed for you, even though it may be distasteful to you; but it may well be that you dislike something even though it is good for you, and it may well be that you love something that is harmful for you; and God knows, while you know not.

They will ask you about fighting during the sacred month. Say, "Fighting during it is a grievous thing, but denying people access to the Way of God, and denying the Divine Reality, and access to the Sacred Place of Prostration—and driving out its people from it—is more grievous in the sight of God; for oppression is worse than war. They won't stop battling you until they turn you away from faith, if they can; and if any of you turns away from his/her faith and dies in denial, their efforts will bear no fruit in this world, nor in the Hereafter—they will become companions of the fire, there to abide.

Truly, those who have faith and those who have renounced evil and are striving in God's Way—they have the hope of God's Infinite Compassion—for God is Oft-Forgiving, Continually Merciful.

They will ask you about intoxicants and gambling. Say, "In both there is great harm and also some benefit for people, but the harm they cause is greater than the gain. And they will ask you about what they should spend (on others). Say, "More than what is due." In this way God makes clear His/Her messages to you that you might reflect—

for this world and the Hereafter. And they will ask you about orphans. Say, "To do that which sets things right and is honest is best." And if your affairs become intermixed—(regard) them as your own siblings; for God distinguishes between one who spoils things and one who makes things better. And if God had willed, He/She could have given you difficulties. Indeed, He/She is Almighty, Truly Wise.

And do not marry idolatrous women (who set other things up in importance before God), until they find tranquility and security in faith. For any faithful servant (of God) is better than a woman who ascribes divinity to other than the Divine Reality, even though she may please you greatly. And do not give women in marriage to men who set other things up in importance before God, before they find faith, for a faithful servant is better than a man who ascribes divinity to other than the Divine Reality, even though he may please you greatly—these draw you into the fire, whereas the Divine Reality draws you into the Garden and forgiveness by Its easing. And He/She makes clear His/Her signs to humankind, so that they might remember.

And they will ask you about the monthly flowings. Say, "It is a vulnerable, painful state. So give women space during their monthly flowings, and do not go in unto them until they are refreshed; and when they are refreshed, go in unto them as God has counselled you." Truly God loves those who turn toward Him/Her; and He/She loves those who purify themselves.

Your women are for you a sustaining wealth; so seek that sustenance as you will, but before you do, prepare— for your soul—be conscious of God, and know that you will come face to face with Him/Her. And share joy with those who have faith.

And do not make God an excuse, as concerns your oaths, against doing good, or acting rightly with conscious awareness, or encouraging peace among people; for God is All-Hearing, All-Knowing.

God will not call you to account for oaths you have voiced impulsively, but for the intention your hearts hold, for God is Oft-Forgiving, Most Forbearing.

For those who have made an oath of being apart from their women, a waiting of four moons is prescribed, but if they return, God is Oft-Forgiving, Infinitely Merciful.

If, however, they are intent upon divorce, God is All-Hearing, All-Knowing.

And women who have been freed from their bond shall wait in regard to themselves for three moons. It is not lawful for them to conceal what God has created in their wombs, if they trust in God and the Day of the Hereafter—and their husbands have the right to take them back during that period if their husbands gently seek peace and reconciliation. The women shall have the same rights to the rights of the men, according to what is equitable, but men have a greater (responsibility) in regard to them; and God is All-Powerful, the Infinitely Wise Healer.

A divorce may be invoked twice, after which the marriage must be resumed in fairness or dissolved in a good way. It is not lawful for you to take back any of what you have ever given to your women, unless both (partners) are concerned they may not be able to keep to the bounds set by God; and so if you fear that either may not be able to keep within the bounds set by God, there shall be no sin for either if the wife gives back (what was gifted) in exchange for her release from bond (from her husband). These are the bounds set by God, so do not transgress them; for they who transgress the bounds set by God—it is they, they who are the wrong-doers.

And if he divorces her (a third time), she shall not be lawful unto him again until after she has married another man, and then if those divorce, there shall be no sin upon either if the (first couple) return to each other— provided they both consider that they will be able to keep within the bounds set by God—for these are the bounds set by God which He/She makes clear to people of inner knowing.

And so, when you divorce women and they approach the end of their term of waiting, then either keep them in a just manner, or let them go in a just manner. But do not keep them against their will to hurt them—for he who does so sins against himself. Do not take these messages of God lightly, and remember the blessings with which God has graced you, and all the Revelation and the wisdom He/She has bestowed upon you from on high through which to counsel you. And remain conscious of God, and know that God has full knowledge of everything.

And when you do divorce women, and they have come to the end of their waiting term, do not keep them from marrying other men if they have committed to each other in a just manner. This is a warning to all of you who have faith in God and the Final Day; it is the most virtuous way, and the purest. And the Divine Reality knows while you do not.

And mothers (who have been divorced) may nurse their children for two whole years, if they wish to complete the time of nursing; and it is incumbent upon he who has begotten the child to provide (during that time) in a just way for their sustenance and clothing. No human being shall be burdened with more than he or she is well able to bear; neither shall a mother be made to suffer because of her child, nor because of his child he who has begotten it. And the same obligation remains with his (the father's) heir. And if both (parents) decide in mutual consent and counsel, upon weaning (the child from the mother), they will incur no sin in it. And if you decide to entrust your children to foster-mothers (for nursing them), you will incur no sin, provided you ensure the security, in a just way, of the child you hand over. But remain conscious of God, and know that the Divine Reality sees all that you do.

If any of you die and leave a spouse behind, they shall wait in regard to themselves for four moons and ten days. When they have fulfilled their time, there is no blame if they bestow themselves in a wise and knowing way. And God is well aware of all that you do.

And there is no blame for you if you make an offer of betrothal, or hold it in your heart—God knows how you cherish them in your hearts—but do not make a secret contract with them unless you do so honorably; and do not commit to the tie of marriage until the prescribed period is completed. And know that God knows what is in your hearts, and take heed of Him/Her, and know that God is Oft-Forgiving, Continually Merciful.

You incur no sin if you divorce women while you have still not touched them or settled a dower upon them, but even then, make provision for them—the wealthy according to his means and he of tight finances according to his means—a provision in an equitable manner: this is an obligation upon all who would do the good.

And if you divorce them before having touched them, but after having settled a dower upon them, then (give them) half of what you have settled upon them, unless they forego their claim, or he in whose hand is the marriage tie gives up his claim (to his half). And to forgo what is due you is more in accord with God-consciousness. And do not forget grace towards each other; truly, God sees all that you do!

Cherish your prayers with vigilance, for in prayer is the best of balance—and stand before God in whole-hearted devotion.

And if you are frightened, troubled by danger, pray while walking or riding, and when you are again secure and tranquil, remember [*zhikr*] God as He/She has taught you, that you did not know.

And if any die and leave spouses behind, it is understood that they bequeath to their widows at least a year's maintenance without their being compelled to depart; if however they depart on their own, there is no error in whatever they may choose to do in regard to themselves, when held high in discernment—and God is Almighty, Most Dear, the Infinitely Wise Healer [*al-ʿAziz, al-Hakim*].

And divorced women shall, also, have maintenance in a goodly manner—this (provision) is incumbent upon all who are conscious of God.

In this way Divine Reality makes clear Its signs to you, that you might use your reason.

Aren't you aware of those who had to forsake their homes in the thousands, in fear of death— and God said to them, "Die." And yet then He/She restored them to life. For the Divine Reality is full of gifts for humankind, but most of them are ungrateful.

Then struggle to know (the flowing fountain of) the Way of God, and know that God hears and knows all things.

And who is it who will loan to God a beautiful loan, which God will double and multiply many times over? It is the Divine Reality who bestows constricted need or expanded abundance, and to It you will return.

Aren't you aware of those elders of the descendants of Israel, after the time of Moses, how they said to a prophet of theirs, "Raise up a king; we will fight in God's Way"? And he (Prophet Samuel) responded, "And if fighting is asked of you, might you perhaps refrain from that effort?" They answered, "And why would we not fight in God's Way, when we have been driven from our homelands?" Yet when struggle was asked of them, they turned back, except for a few of them; but God has full knowledge of those who do harm.

And their prophet spoke to those elders: "God has raised up Saul [*Talut*] now to be your king." They responded, "How can he rule over us when we have a better right to rule than he, and he has no great wealth?" He replied, "See—God has raised him up above you, and endowed him with abundant knowledge and physical perfection. And God bestows His/Her dominion on whom He/She wills, for God is Infinite, All-Knowing."

And their prophet (continued) to speak to them, "Behold, it shall be a sign of his rightful dominion that you will be granted the Ark (of the Covenant—a heart) endowed by your Sustainer with tranquility [*sakinah*, "inner peace"] and with all that is enduring in the angel-borne heritage left behind by the House of Moses and the House of Aaron. In this indeed is a sign for you if you are of the faithful.

When Saul set forth with the forces, he said, "God will test you with the river. Whoever drinks of the water, he is not of me. For truly, those who do not drink of it—except a handful—are of me." Yet all but a few drank of it greedily. When they had crossed the river, he and the faithful ones with him, they (the faint-hearted ones) said, "We have no strength today against Goliath and his forces." But those who knew with certainty that they would meet God replied, "How often has a small host overcome a great host by God's permission, for God is with those who are patient in adversity."

And when they came face to face with Goliath and his forces, they prayed, "O our Sustainer, shower us with patience in adversity, and make our steps firm, and support us when we face people who are in denial of Truth."

By God's will, they overcame them, and David slew Goliath; and God gave him authority and wisdom and taught him what He/She willed. And if God did not restrain one group of people by means of another the earth would be full of corruption. But the Divine Reality is limitless in beneficence towards all the worlds.

These are the Signs of Divine Reality. We declare them to you in Truth [*bil Haqq*]. Truly, you are one of the Message bearers.

Such Messengers We endowed with gifts, some above others. To some Divine Reality spoke; others He/She raised in degrees (of honor). To Jesus the son of Mary We gave clear Signs and strengthened him with the Holy Spirit [*Ruh al-Quddus*]. If God had so willed, further generations would not have argued with each other, after clear Signs had come to them, but they chose to quarrel, some having faith and others denying. If Divine Reality

40

had so willed, they would not have disputed with each other, but Divine Reality fulfills Its design.

O you who have faith, spend on others out of the bounties We have provided for you, before the Day comes when no bargaining, nor friendship, nor intercession (will avail). Those who cover over Truth, they are the ones in darkness.

God—there is no deity but *Hu*, the Ever-Living, the Self-Subsisting Source of all Being. No slumber can seize Him/Her nor sleep. All things in heaven and on earth belong to *Hu*. Who could intercede in His/Her Presence without His/Her permission? He/She knows what appears in front of and behind His/Her creatures. Nor can they encompass any knowledge of Him/Her except what He/She wills. His/Her throne extends over the heavens and the earth, and He/She feels no fatigue in guarding and preserving them, for He/She is the Highest and Most Exalted. [*Allahu la ilaha illa Huwa al-Hayy al-Qayyum, la ta'khudhuhu sinatun wa la nawm. Lahu ma fis-samawati wa ma fil 'ardi. Man zhallazhi yashfa'u 'indahu illa bi izhnihi. Ya'lamu ma bayna aydihim wa ma khalfahum wa la yuhituna bishay'in min 'ilmihi illa bima sha'a. Wasi'a kursi-yyuhus-samawati wal 'ard, wa la ya'uduhu hifdhuhuma wa Hu wal-'Aliyy al-'Azim.*]

Let there be no compulsion in matters of faith. Right wayfaring stands clearly apart from error. Whoever turns away from the powers of evil and has faith in Divine Reality has grasped the most trustworthy handhold which shall never give way. And Divine Reality is All-Hearing, All-Knowing.

Divine Reality is the Protector of those who have faith, leading them out of the depths of darkness into the Light. Whereas near to those who turn away from

41

the Truth are the powers of evil that take them out of
the light into the depths of darkness. It is they who are
destined for the fire, there to abide.

Are you not aware of he who argued with Abraham
about his Sustainer, because God had gifted him with
kingship? Witness, Abraham said, "My Sustainer is the
One Who Gifts Life, and the One Who Gifts Death."
The king replied, "I gift life and gift death!" Abraham
said, "God causes the sun to rise in the east. Make it rise,
then, in the west." And he who was intent on denying
Truth was dumbfounded. For God does not guide people
who are arrogantly unjust.

Or (are you) like one who passed by a town deserted
by its people, with its roofs fallen in, saying "How could
God bring all this back to life after its demise?" And so
God caused him to be as dead for a hundred years, and
then brought him back to life, saying, "How long have
you remained so?" And he answered, "I have remained
but a day or part of a day." Said (the Divine Reality):
"No, you have remained like this a hundred years! But
look at your food and drink—see how it is untouched by
the passing of years, and your ass; that We might make
of you a Sign for humankind. And observe bones of
animals and human beings—how We arrange them and
clothe them with flesh." And when he had observed all
this, he said, "I comprehend now that God has the power
to will anything!"

And witness, Abraham said, "O my Sustainer! Show
me how You give life to the dead." Said *Hu*, "Do you
not have faith?" Abraham answered, "Yes, but so that
my heart might be completely secure, at rest." Said *Hu*,
"Take then four birds and teach them to come close to
you; then place them separately on hills; then summon

42

them—they will come flying to you. And know that God is Almighty, Truly Wise."

The parable of those who spend their possessions in God's Way is like a seed that sends forth seven ears, in each of which are a hundred grains. For God grants manifold increase to whom He/She wills. And Divine Reality is Infinite, All-Encompassing and All-Knowing.

Those who spend their possessions for the sake of God, and do not follow their spending with a show of their beneficence nor embarrassment (of the one to whom they gave), shall have their recompense with their Sustainer. And no fear need they have, and neither shall they grieve.

A kind word and the veiling of another's want is better than a charitable deed followed by hurt. And God is Self-Sufficient, Most Forbearing.

O you who have faith! Don't nullify your charity by stressing your benevolence and hurting (the feelings of those to whom you give) as does one who spends his wealth only to be seen by people and has no faith in the Divine Reality and the Final Day: for his parable is like that of a hard rock with little earth upon it—then a rainstorm hits it and leaves it hard and bare. Such as these shall have no gain from all their efforts, for God does not guide people who deny the Truth.

And the parable of those who spend that which they are provided out of a longing for God to be well-pleased with them, and from out of their own inner certainty and nearness, is that of a garden on high, fertile ground—a rainstorm pours down upon it, and it brings forth redoubled fruitfulness; and if no rainstorm pours down upon it, light dew (arrives and is enough). And God sees all that you do.

Would any of you like to have a garden with date-palms and vineyards, through which running waters flow and all kinds of fruit abound within it, and then be overwhelmed by old age with only incapable children to look after it, and then have it be struck by fiery wind and completely scorched?! And so, God makes clear His/Her messages to you, so that you might reflect.

O you who have faith! Spend on others out of the good things you may have acquired, and out of that which We bring forth for you out of the earth; and do not choose for your charity the worst which you yourselves would not accept without diverting your eyes in disdain. And know that God is the One Who Is Truly Rich, the One Worthy of all Praise [*al-Ghani, al-Hamid*].

Satan threatens you with the prospect of poverty and bids you to be stingy, while the Divine Reality promises you forgiveness and abundance. And God is Infinite, All-Encompassing, All-Knowing [*al-Wasi, al-'Alim*];

He/She grants wisdom to whom He/She wills, and whoever is granted wisdom has indeed been granted abundant wealth, but none bears this in mind except those who are gifted with insight.

For whatever you may spend (on others) or whatever you may vow (to spend), truly, God knows it; and those who do wrong (by withholding) shall have none to support them.

And if you do deeds of charity openly, it is a blessing; but if you bestow it upon those truly in need in secret, it is even better for you, and it will rebalance some of the harm you have done. And God is well aware of all that you do.

It is not for you to make people follow a rightful path, since it is God alone who guides whom He/She wills.

And whatever of good you spend on others is for your own good, provided that you spend only out of a longing for the Face of Divine Reality. For whatever of good you may spend will be given back to you in full, and you shall not be wronged.

(And give) to the needy who, absorbed in God's cause, are unable to go about the earth (in search of livelihood). One who is lacking in awareness may think that they are free of want, because of their modesty—you can recognize them by their exceptional mark, they do not insistently go about begging of everyone. And whatever of good you may give, surely God knows.

Those who spend their possessions (for God's sake) by night and by day, secretly and openly, shall have their reward with their Sustainer. No fear need they have, neither shall they grieve.

Those who stuff themselves with usury behave as those whom Satan has confused with his touch; for they say, "Buying and selling is just a kind of usury, but God has made buying and selling lawful but usury unlawful!" And so whoever becomes aware of his or her Sustainer's admonition and desists may keep his or her past gains, and it will be for God to judge; but as for those who return to it—they are destined for the fire, there to abide.

God deprives usurious gain of blessing, whereas He/ She causes charitable giving to increase with interest. And God does not love anyone who is stubbornly un-grateful and persists in corrupt ways.

Truly those who have come to faith and do the deeds of wholeness and reconciliation, and are constant in prayer, and bestow charity—they shall have their reward with their Sustainer. No fear need they have, and neither shall they grieve.

45

O you who have come to faith, remain conscious of the Divine Reality. And give up all that remains of usury, if you are of the faithful.

For if you don't, know that you are in conflict with God and His Messenger. But if you repent in your ways, you are entitled to your principal; you will do no wrong, neither will you be wronged.

If however, the debtor is in tightened circumstances, (grant him or her) a delay until it is easy. And it would be for your own good—if you but knew it—to forego it (entirely) out of charity.

And be in awe of the Day you will return to God and every soul will be repaid for what he or she has earned, and none shall be wronged.

O you who have faith, whenever you give or take credit for a certain term, put it down in writing. And let a scribe write it clearly and equitably between you; and let not the scribe refuse to write, as God has taught him—even so shall he write. And let the one who is taking on the debt dictate, and let him be conscious of God, his Sustainer, and not diminish anything of what he undertakes. And if he is weak in body, or mind, or not able to dictate himself, let the one who oversees his affairs dictate justly. And call upon two among your men as witnesses, and if two men are not available, then a man and two women of those with whom you are well-pleased as witnesses, so that if one should become confounded, the other might guide in recollection. And let the witnesses not refuse to give evidence when they are called. And do not be reluctant to write down every contractual detail, be it small or great, noting the time when it falls due; this is more just in the sight of God, more straightforward as evidence, and more likely to keep you from being doubtful regarding it. If however ready merchandise is concerned—which you transfer directly from one to another—you won't be transgressing if you don't write it down. And have witnesses whenever you engage in trade with each other, but do not pressure either scribe or witness—for if you do, you would be going beyond bounds—and remain conscious of God, since it is through God that you come to know, and God has full knowledge of everything.

And if you are on a journey and cannot find a scribe, pledge in trust hand to hand—and if you thus deposit a trust with one another, then let the one who takes on a trust fulfill it, and let him be conscious of God, his Sustainer. And do not cover over what you have witnessed—for truly one who conceals it, his heart goes astray—and God knows well all that you do.

Unto God belongs all that is in the heavens and all that is on earth. And whether you reveal what is within yourselves or conceal it, God will call you to account for it; and then He/She will forgive whom He/She wills, and will chastise whom He/She wills: for God has the power to will anything.

The Messenger and the faithful with him have faith in what has been revealed to him from on high by his Sustainer; they all have faith in God, and His angels, and His Revelations, and His Messengers, making no distinction between any of His Messengers. And they say, "We have heard and we pay heed. Grant us Your forgiveness, O our Sustainer, for with You is all journeys' end.

"Divine Reality does not burden any human being with more than he or she can bear; in his or her favor shall be whatever good he or she does, and against him or her whatever harm he or she does. O You Who Sustain

47

and Educate us, do not take us to task if we forget or un-wittingly do wrong. O our Sustainer, do not lay upon us a burden like that which You placed upon those who lived before us. O our Sustainer, do not make us bear burdens which we do not have the strength to bear. And clear us of our errors, and grant us forgiveness, and bestow Your mercy upon us. You are our Supreme Cherisher and Protector; help us, then, when we face those who stand against Truth."

Al-ʿImran

(The House of ʿImran)

In the Name of God, the Infinitely Compassionate,
the Continually Merciful

Alif. Lam. Mim.

God—there is no deity but *Hu*, the Ever-Living, the Self-Subsistent, Eternal Source of All Being. [*Allahu, la illaha illa Huwa, al-Hayy, al-Qayyum.*]

Step by step it is He/She who has sent down to you this Book, within Truth [*bil Haqq*], confirming what remains of earlier Revelation; for it is He/She who bestowed the Torah and the Gospel,

before, as a guidance to humankind—it is He/She who has sent down the criterion for discerning right from wrong. Witness how grievous suffering comes to those who are bent on denying God's Signs—for Divine Reality is Almighty, the Rectifier of Wrongs.

Truly, nothing on earth or in the heavens is hidden from God.

It is He/She who forms and prepares you in the wombs as He/She wills. There is no Reality but He/She, the Almighty, the Truly Wise [*al-ʿAziz, al-Hakim*].

It is He/She who has sent down to you from on high this Book. Within it are signs [*ayat* (verses)] firmly rooted—these are the "Mother of the Book" [*Umm al-Kitab* (the life-giving and nourishing essence of the

Revelation)]—and others that are similar (in allegory like those that came before). Those whose hearts stray into confusion chase after the parts that are similar, pursuing discord and their interpretations. But no one fully knows its ultimate, complete meaning but God. And so, those deeply-rooted in knowledge say: "We have faith in it— the whole of it is from our Sustainer; though none grasp the remembrance [y*azh-zhakkaru*] except those of tender heart and discerning insight.

"O our Sustainer, do not let our hearts swerve from the Truth, after You have guided us, and from Your Presence, gift us with compassion. Truly, You are the Giver of Gifts! [*Rabbana, la tuzhigh quloobana ba'ada izh hadaytana wahab lana min ladunka rahmatan innaka anta al-Wahhab.*]

"O our Sustainer, truly You will gather humankind together to witness the Day, about which there is no doubt. Truly God never fails to fulfill His/Her Promise."

Witness those who deny the Truth—neither their possessions, nor their offspring will be of help to them facing Divine Reality. It is those (their attachments) that are kindling for the fire.

Similar to what happened to Pharaoh's people, and those who lived before them—they denied Our messages, and so Divine Reality called them to account for their errors; for Divine Reality is stringent in rectifying, step by step.

Say to those who deny Truth, "You are bound to be overcome and gathered into the abode of fire—how distressful a resting-place."

You've already had a Sign in the two groups facing each other—one striving in the Way of God, the other denying. With their own eyes, they (those striving) saw twice their number, but God strengthens with His support whom He/She wills; indeed, witness: in this is a lesson for all who have eyes to see.

Beautiful in the eyes of men is the love of things they desire—women and children, piles of gold and silver, horses of high mark, and cattle, and land—such are the pleasures of the life of this world; but nearness with God is the most beautiful aspiration to achieve.

Say: "Shall I give you tidings of what is better than those? For the God-conscious, there are with their Sustainer gardens with waters running through—there is their eternal home, with pure spouses and the good pleasure of God." For within the sight of God are His/Her servants—

those who say: "O our Sustainer! Witness, we have faith and keep the trust; forgive us our errors and protect us from suffering through the fire!"—

those who patiently persevere in adversity and are true to their word, and are truly devoted, and who spend in God's Way, and pray for forgiveness from their innermost hearts before dawn.

God bears witness, as do the angels and all who are endowed with knowledge, that there is no reality but *Hu*, the Upholder of Justice; there is no deity but *Hu*, the Almighty, the Truly Wise Healer.

Witness, the only religion with God is self-surrender. Nor did those who were earlier entrusted with Revelation diverge from that until corruption among themselves (drove them into separation), after knowledge had already come to them; but for those who deny God's Messages, witness, Divine Reality is swift in Reckoning.

So if they argue with you, say, "I have surrendered my whole being to Divine Reality; I and those who follow me." And ask those who have earlier been entrusted with Revelation, as well as those who are without any, "Have you surrendered yourselves to That?" And if they do surrender themselves to It, they are directly guided, but if they turn away—witness, your responsibility is only to convey the Message. For God clearly sees all that is within His/Her creatures.

Truly, as for those who cover over the Signs of Divine Reality [*Ayati Allahi*], and kill the exalted prophets, contrary to all that is true and rightful, and kill people who encourage balance and justice—make them aware of a painful chastisement.

It is they whose deeds will bear no fruit, in this world or the Hereafter; and they shall have none to support them.

Haven't you seen those who have been given a share of Revelation before, who have been invited to let it be their guide when disputes arise, and yet some stubbornly turn away?

This because they say, "The fire shall not touch us but a few numbered days." How their delusions have caused them to stray from their faith!

How then will it be when We gather them all together to witness the Day about which there is no doubt, and every soul is repaid in full for what he or she has done, and none are wronged?

Say: "Divine Reality, Supreme Sovereign of all dominions! You grant dominion to whom You will, and remove dominion from whom You will; and You exalt whom You will, and bring low whom You will. In Your touch is all good. Truly, You have the power to will anything.

"You cause the night to enter through the day, and You cause the day to enter through the night. And You bring forth the living out of that which is dead, and You bring forth the dead out of that which is living. And You grant sustenance to whom You will, beyond all reckoning!" [*Wa tarzuqu man tashaa'u bi ghayri hisaab.*]

Let not the faithful take those who cover over the Truth as friends and supporters in preference to the faithful—for one who does so cuts himself or herself off from Divine Reality—unless you fear from them something to be guarded against and in this way avert it. But Divine Reality Itself cautions you to be vigilant— and to God is the final goal, the return [*wa ila Allahi al-maseer*].

Say: "Whether you conceal what is in your hearts or reveal it, God knows it, for He/She knows all that is in the heavens and all that is on earth, and God has the power to will anything. [*Wa yaalamu ma fee as-samawati wama fee al-ardi wallahu aala kulli shay-in qadeer.*]

"On the Day when every soul will be faced with all the good it has done and with all the harm it has done, many a soul will wish there had been a long span of time between it and that Day. And so Divine Reality Itself cautions you (to be mindful); and God is most tender towards His/Her servants."

Say: "If you do love God, align with my Path. God will love you and forgive you your errors, for Divine Reality is Oft-Forgiving, Infinitely Merciful [*al-Ghafur, ar-Rahim*]."

Say: "Willingly align with Divine Reality and Its Messenger"; but if they turn away—God does not love those who ungratefully cover over Truth.

Truly, God chose Adam, and Noah, the family of Abraham, and the family of 'Imran for the sake of all the worlds, offspring, one from the other, and, surely, God is All-Hearing, All-Knowing.

Behold, the woman of 'Imran said, "O my Sustainer! I dedicate to You what is in my womb for Your special service: so, accept this of me; for, truly, You are the All-Hearing and All-Knowing [*as-Sami, al-'Alim*]."

But when she had given birth, she said, "O my Sustainer! Behold, I have given birth to a girl"—all the while, Divine Reality was well-aware of that to which she would give birth, and that no male child could be like this female—"and I have named her Mary. And, truly, I seek Your protection for her and her offspring from Satan, the corrupt and scorned."

And so, facing her with favor, her Sustainer accepted her, and made her to grow in beautiful purity, and placed her under the care of Zachariah. Whenever Zachariah visited her in the sanctuary [*mihrab*], he found sustenance there with her. He would ask, "O Mary, from where does this come to you?" She would answer, "It is from God. See how Divine Reality provides sustenance for whom He/She wills, beyond all reckoning!" [*Inna Allaha yarzuqu man yashaa'u bighayri hisaab.*]

It was there Zachariah prayed to his Sustainer, "O my Sustainer! From Yourself grant me offspring that is pure, for You are the One who Hears prayer."

While he was standing in prayer there in the sanctuary [*mihrab*], the angels called unto him, "Divine Reality gives you glad tidings of *Yahya* ["the Living One"], who shall witness to the truth of a Word from Divine Reality, and be upright and noble, and chaste, and a prophet, of the company of those who do the sound deeds of wholeness and reconciliation."

Zachariah exclaimed, "How can I have a son when I

am very old and my wife is barren?" "Thus it is," was the answer, "God accomplishes what He/She wills."

Zachariah said, "O my Sustainer! Grant me a Sign!" The answer came: "Your Sign shall be that for three days you shall not speak to anyone except through gestures. Then remember [*zhikr*] your Sustainer abundantly, and glorify Him/Her through the evening and through the morning."

And behold, the angels said, "O Mary, God has chosen you and purified you—chosen you above all women of all worlds.

"O Mary! Devotedly serve your Sustainer. Prostrate [*asjudi (sajdah)*] and bow down [*arka'ee (ruku)*] with those who bow [*ar-raaki'een*]."

This account of something unseen, that was beyond the reach of your perception, We reveal to you—for you were not with them when they cast arrows to see which of them should be Mary's guardian, nor were you with them when they argued about it.

Behold! The angels said, "O Mary, God gives you glad tidings of a Word from Him—his name will be Christ ('the Anointed') Jesus, the son of Mary [*Al Maseehu Aeesa ibnu Maryama*], held in honor in this world and Hereafter, and of those near to God.

"He will speak to the people in childhood and in maturity, and shall be of those who do the deeds of wholeness and reconciliation."

She said, "O my Sustainer! How can I have a son when no man has ever touched me?" He answered: "Thus it is; God creates what He wills. When He gives power to a thing to be, He but says unto it, 'Be!'—and it is. [*Kun—fa yakun.*]

"And Divine Reality will impart knowledge of the

Book to him, and wisdom, the Torah, and the Gospel.

"And as a Messenger (he will say) to the descendants of Israel: 'I have come to you with a Sign from your Sustainer—I shall create for you out of seeming clay the figure of a bird and breathe into it, and, by permission of Divine Reality, it shall become a bird flying with love. And I shall heal the blind and the lepers, and I will bring the dead back to life, by permission of Divine Reality. And I shall tell you of what you may eat and what you might gather within your houses. Surely in all that is a Sign for you if you might have faith.

"'And to declare the Truth of that which came clearly before, of the Torah, and to open as lawful to you a portion of what was prohibited for you; I have come to you with a Sign from your Sustainer, so be attentive, conscious of Divine Reality, and be in alignment with me.

"'It is Divine Reality who is my Sustainer, and your Sustainer—so worship and serve It. This is a straightforward and open Way.'"

And when Jesus became aware of their denial of the Truth, he said, "Who will be my helpers in the Way of God?" The white-garbed ones [*al-hawariyyun*, "the purified"] responded, "We will be helpers of God. We trust in Divine Reality; be our witness that to It we are surrendered [*muslimun*].

"O our Sustainer and Educator, we trust in the Revelation You have bestowed from on high, and we walk in the way of the Messenger. Make us one with all those who bear witness (to Truth)."

And (the deniers) plotted and planned, but Divine Reality also planned, and God is the best of planners.

Behold, Divine Reality said, "O Jesus! Truly, I will fulfill My Promise to you and raise you to Myself, and clear you of those who ungratefully deny the Truth. I will make those who follow you higher than those who turn away from Truth, unto the Day of Resurrection. You are all returning to Me, and I will judge between you in regard to all that about which you would dispute.

"And as for those who are determined to deny the Truth, I will purify them with an intense suffering in this world and the Hereafter, and they will have none to help them,

"whereas those who have faith and do the deeds of wholeness and reconciliation, Divine Reality will grant them full recompense; for God does not love those who do harm.

"This is what We declare to you from among the Signs [*Ayat*], and of the Infinitely Wise Recitation of Remembrance [*wa-zhikri al-hakim*]."

Truly, with God, the likeness of Jesus is as the likeness of Adam, whom He created out of dust and then said unto him: "Be!"—and he is [*Kun—fa yakun*].

The Truth is from your Sustainer, so do not be of those in doubt.

And if anyone should argue with you about this, now after all the knowledge that has come to you, say: "Come! Let us call together our children and your children, and our women and your women, and ourselves and your-selves, and then let us humbly and earnestly pray, and ask that those who speak falsely might be disinherited of the mercy and blessings of God."

Behold, this is the story of Truth [*al-qasasu al-Haqq*]— there is no god but God; Divine Reality—It alone is the Almighty, Most Dear, the Truly Wise, Who Renders All Sound.

And if they turn away, behold—God knows full well

those who spread corruption.

Say: "O people of the Book, come to the principle that is common among us [*kalimatin sawa'in*, 'common word']: that we worship and serve none but Divine Reality; that we do not ascribe Divinity to anything besides That, and that we shall not take from among ourselves anyone as our Lord and Sustainer, anyone other than God." And if they turn away, say, "Bear witness that (to God) we are surrendered [*muslimun*]."

O people of the Book! Why do you argue about Abraham—when the Torah and the Gospel were not revealed until after him? Will you not use your reason?

See how you argue even about things you know; why do you argue about that of which you have no knowledge? Yet Divine Reality knows, while you do not know.

Abraham was neither "a Jew" nor "a Christian," but was one who truly turned away from all that is false [*al-hanif*], having surrendered himself to Divine Reality, and he was not of those who ascribe divinity to anything other than It.

Surely, among humankind the closest to Abraham are those who follow in his footsteps—as also does this Prophet and the faithful—and Divine Reality is the protective Friend near to those who have faith [*wallahu Waliyyu al-mu'mineen*].

Some of the people of the Book would like to lead you astray, but it is themselves they lead astray; yet they do not perceive it.

O people of the Book! Why do you deny the Messages of Divine Reality when you yourselves bear witness to them?

O people of the Book! Why do you confuse Truth with falsehood and conceal the Truth when you know?

Some of the people of the Book say, "Acknowledge in the morning your belief in what has been revealed to those who are faithful, but deny the truth of it later on, so that they might turn back from it;

"and do not trust in anyone unless he or she follows your religion." Say: "Behold! True guidance is God's guidance. (Are you afraid) that a revelation might be sent to someone else like the revelation that was sent to you? Or that they might then engage you in debate about Divine Reality?" Say: "Behold! All bounties are in the hand of God who bestows them on whom He/She wills. And God is All-Encompassing in His/Her care and is All-Knowing [*al-Wasi, al-'Alim*],

choosing for His/Her Compassion whom He/She wills. And Divine Reality is Infinite in Its Great Bounty."

And among the people of the Book there is many a one who if you entrust him or her with a treasure of gold will restore it fully to you; and there are others among them who if you entrust them with even a small piece of silver will not restore it to you, unless you keep standing over them—which is the result of their assertion that, "No blame is ours in regard to these unknowing people"—and so they speak a lie about Divine Reality, even though they are well aware.

No! But those who keep their bond with Him and keep conscious of Him—truly, God loves those who are conscious of Him [*Allaha yuhibbu al-muttaqeen*].

See how those who trade their bond with God, and their promises, for a trifling gain—they shall have no portion of the blessings of the life to come, and God will not speak with them nor look at them on the Day of Recognition; nor will Divine Reality clear them of their errors—theirs shall be a painful suffering.

59

And witness how there are some among them who twist the Revelation with their tongues, so as to make you think that it's a part of the Revelation, but it is not part of the Revelation: and they say, "This is from God," while it is not from God. It is they who tell a lie about Divine Reality; and they know it.

It isn't conceivable that a person to whom is given Revelation and wisdom and the responsibility of prophethood should say to people, "Worship me beside Divine Reality," but instead, "Be devoted servants of the One who cherishes and educates you!"—for you would have taught the Revelation and studied it wholeheartedly.

Nor would he teach you to take angels and prophets as your Sustainer—would he counsel you to deny the Truth after you have surrendered yourself to Divine Reality?

And see how God took hold of the bond with the prophets, saying: "I give you the Book and wisdom; then if there comes to you a messenger, confirming what is with you, trust in him and help him. Do you acknowledge and take this My Covenant as binding for you?" They responded, "We give our pledge." He said, "Then bear witness, and I am among you as witness."

And from now on, all who turn away, it is they who wander into confusion.

Do they seek other than the Way of Divine Reality? While all creatures in the heavens and on earth have willingly or unwillingly surrendered—and to Him/Her they all are returning.

Say: "We have faith in Divine Reality, and in what has been revealed to us, and what was revealed to Abraham, Isma'il, Isaac, Jacob, and the Tribes, and in that given to Moses, Jesus, and all the prophets from their Sustainer and Cherisher, and we make no distinction between them, and to God we bow in surrender."

If anyone desires a Way other than Surrender, never will it be confirmed for him or her, and in the Hereafter he/she will be among those who are lost.

How shall God guide those who turn away in denial, after having accepted faith and borne witness to the Messenger of Truth and clear Signs that had come to them? For God does not guide a people who cover themselves in darkness.

Their recompense is that they are driven away from God's blessings, and those of His/Her angels, and of the gathering of humanity.

In this state they abide, nor will their suffering be lightened, nor will they find any relief;

but excepted shall be those who turn around and reorient themselves—for see how Divine Reality is Oft-Forgiving, Infinitely Merciful [*al-Ghafur, ar-Rahim*].

Truly, as for those who cover over the Truth after having come to trust, and then become even more stubborn in their denial, for them turning will not be recognized, for they will have lost their way in confusion.

Truly, as for those who are determined to deny the Truth and die as deniers, not even all the gold on earth could deliver them. It is they who are in painful suffering, and have none to help in support.

You will never attain true Goodness [*al-birra, al-Barr*] unless you bestow on others of what you yourselves truly love; and whatever you give, certainly, God knows.

All food was lawful to the children of Israel, except what Israel (Jacob) had rendered unlawful to himself, before the Torah was revealed from on high. Say, "Bring the Torah then, and follow it, if what you say is true."

And all who make up falsehoods about Divine Reality after this—it is they who are the harm-doers.

Say: "God speaks the Truth. So follow the Way of Abraham, who turned away from all that is false, and was not of those who attributed Divinity to anything besides Divine Reality."

Behold, the first sanctuary established for humanity was indeed the one at Bakkah, rich in blessing and of guidance to all the worlds,

full of clear Signs, the station (*maqam*) of Abraham—and whoever enters it finds security and inner peace—and so for all people who are able to undertake it, let pilgrimage to the House (*al-Bayt*: the Kaaba; into the heart) be an endeavor worthy of Divine Reality. And as for those who deny the Truth—truly, Divine Reality is rich without need of anything in all the worlds.

Say: "O People of the Book, why do you deny the signs of Divine Reality, when Divine Reality bears witness to all that you do?"

Say: "O People of the Book, why do you obstruct the path of those who have faith by making it appear as though it is crooked, when you, yourselves, bear witness to it? For Divine Reality is not unaware of all that you do."

O you who have faith, if you were to pay attention to a faction of the People of the Book they might cause you to turn back from faith to denial.

And how could you deny the Truth when God's Signs are being conveyed to you and His Messenger is living among you? Whoever holds firmly, steadfastly to Divine Reality is guided to a clear Path.

O you who have faith, be conscious of Divine Reality with true, real consciousness, and do not let death overtake you, before you have surrendered your selves to It.

And hold fast, all together, to the rope of God, and do not separate from one another. And remember with gratitude the blessings which God has bestowed on you: how, when you were adversaries, He brought your hearts together, so that through His blessings you became as though of one family; and how when you were on the brink of a fiery abyss, He saved you from it. In this way, God makes clear His/Her Signs to you, so that you might be guided,

and that there might grow out of you a community who invite to all that is good, and encourage the doing of what is known to be good and restrain the doing of what is wrongful: and it is they who shall attain felicity!

And do not be like those who draw apart from one another and succumb to arguing even after clear Signs have come to them—for these there is a mighty anguish

on the Day when some faces will be bright and others endarkened. As for those whose faces are endarkened with sorrow: "Did you reject faith after having known it? Taste, then, this anguish caused by ungratefully turning away in denial."

But those of bright faces, they shall be within God's Compassion [*Rahmati Allahi*], there abiding.

These are the Signs of Divine Reality; We convey them to you, within Truth, since God wills no hurt to any of His/Her creation in all the worlds.

And to God belongs all that is in the heavens and all that is on earth; and all matters are returning to God. [*Wa lillahi ma fee as-samawati wama fee al-ardi wa-ila Allahi turja'au al-umuur.*]

You are the best community brought forth to

humanity (for the benefit of humanity), encouraging what is known to be good, restraining what is harmful, and trusting in the Divine Reality. If only all the people of the Book had such faith, it would be for their benefit—among them are faithful ones, but many are corrupt.

But these can never cause you more than a brief hurt; and if they fight against you, they will turn in flight and will not be helped.

Overshadowed by shame they are where they may be found, except when they are in a covenant with God and with humankind. They draw towards themselves the stringency of God, and over them is pitched (the tent of) humiliation—this because they rejected the Signs of God and killed the prophets in defiance of Truth; this because they rebelled and have transgressed beyond bounds.

But they are not all alike; among the people of the Book there are upright people who recount the Meanings of God throughout the night and prostrate themselves in awe.

They have faith in the Divine Reality and the Day of the Hereafter, and encourage the doing of what is known to be good, and restrain the doing of what is wrongful, and hasten in doing the good: and these are among the righteous.

And of the good they do, they shall never be denied the recompense, for God has full knowledge of those who are conscious of Him/Her.

Those who ungratefully reject faith, neither their possessions nor their children will help them at all when facing Divine Reality; they will be companions of the fire, abiding there.

What they spend on the life of this world is like a wind bringing frost—it strikes the developed land of people who have wronged their own souls and destroys it, for it is not God who wrongs them, but they who wrong their own souls.

O you who have faith, do not take for your intimate friends people who are not like you (who are not of your character). They will keep trying to corrupt you; they love what troubles you. They have already shown forth hatred from their mouths, but what their hearts conceal is worse. We have made clear the Signs to you, if you would but use your understanding.

Indeed, it is you who love them, but they do not love you, even though you have faith in the whole of the Book. When they encounter you, they say, "We have faith," but when they are alone, they gnaw their fingers in their seething resentment against you. Say, "Pass away in your resentment; truly, God knows well the secrets of hearts."

If good fortune comes to you, it grieves them, and if harm befalls you, they rejoice. But if you are patiently persevering in adversity and conscious of God, their guile cannot harm you at all. For truly, God encompasses everything they do.

And remember when you set out from your household in the early morning to arrange the faithful at their stations for battle; and God is All-Hearing, All-Knowing [*as-Sami, al-'Alim*]—

remember when two groups among you were about to lose heart, but God kept them close as their protecting Friend, and it is in God the faithful must place their trust.

For indeed, God supported you at Badr ("Full Moon") when you were utterly weak. Be conscious of God, that you might be among the grateful.

Remember you said to the faithful: "Is it not enough that your Sustainer should help you with three thousand angels pouring down?

"No, if you steadfastly persevere and are conscious of Him, and the enemy suddenly rushes upon you, your Sustainer will aid you with five thousand angels swooping down!"

And God made this known as joyful news for you, that your hearts might be in tranquility—since no help can come from any but God, the Almighty, the Truly Wise [*al-'Aziz, al-Hakim*]—

that He might cut off a part of those who ungratefully deny Truth, or lay them low, that they might turn back, without success.

And it is not for you to decide whether He will accept their repentance or chastise them. For they are indeed those who do wrong (bringing darkness);

to God belongs all that is in the heavens and all that is on earth. He/She forgives whom He/She wills and He/She chastises whom He/She wills; and Divine Reality is Oft-forgiving, Infinitely Merciful [*al-Ghafur, ar-Rahim*].

O you who have faith, do not devour usury, doubled and multiplied many times over; but remain conscious of God, that you may attain felicity.

Guard yourself from the fire that is prepared for those who deny Truth.

And align with Divine Reality and the Messenger, so that you might be graced with Mercy.

And hasten to attain your Sustainer's forgiveness and a paradise as vast as the heavens and the earth, which has been prepared for those who are conscious of God,

who spend (in God's Way) in times of abundance and in times of hardship, and hold in check their anger, and pardon their fellow human beings, for God loves those who do the good and beautiful [*wallahu yuhibbu al-muhsineen*];

and who, when they have committed a shameful deed, or have otherwise wronged their own souls, remember [*zhikr—zhakaru*] Divine Reality [*Allah*] and pray for forgiveness for their mistakes—for who can forgive sins but God?—and do not knowingly persist in doing whatever wrong they may have done.

For such, the reward is forgiveness from their Sustainer and gardens with rivers flowing beneath them, there to abide—how blessed a recompense for those who strive.

Many ways of life have passed away before you. Go, then, about the earth and see what happened in the end to those who denied the Truth;

here is a clear lesson for all human beings, and a guidance and counsel for those who are conscious of God.

So do not lose heart, nor grieve; for if you are faithful you are bound to ascend.

If a wound has touched you, be sure a similar wound has touched others. Continually, We bring such days among people by turns that Divine Reality may know which are of the faithful, and that He/She may take to Himself/Herself witnesses to Truth from among you— for God does not love those who do wrong—

and that God might render pure of any dross those who trust, and bring to nothing those who deny the Truth.

Do you think you could enter the Garden without Divine Reality knowing how you have striven to your utmost and knowing how you are patient in adversity?

For indeed you longed for death before you came face to face with it; and now you have seen it with your own eyes!

And Muhammad is but a Messenger; many Messengers before him have passed on. If he dies or is killed, will that make you turn back on your heels? But one who turns back on his or her heels cannot harm God in the least—Divine Reality will swiftly recompense all who are grateful [*ash-shakireen*].

Nor can a soul die except by permission of Divine Reality, at a term already written. If any desire the rewards of this world, We shall give that to him/her; and if any desire the rewards of the other world We shall give that to him/her. And swiftly We reward those who are grateful.

And how many a prophet has fought, with devoted ones at their side, and they did not lose heart even with all they had to suffer in God's cause, and neither did they weaken, nor did they lower themselves. And God loves those who are patient in adversity.

And all they said was: "O our Sustainer, forgive us our errors, and the lack of moderation in our actions. And make firm our steps, and support us when we face those who deny the Truth,"

and Divine Reality bestowed upon them the rewards of this world, as well as the beautiful rewards of the other world; for God loves those who strive to act with beauty and goodness [*wallahu yuhibbu al-muhsineen*].

O you who have faith, if you align with the deniers, they will turn you back on your heels, and you will turn back to your own loss.

No; it is God who is your Best Protector and Friend, and He/She is the Best of Helpers [*Allahu mawlakum wahuwa khayru an-nasireen*].

We cause trembling fear within the hearts of those who deny the Truth, caused by their ascribing divinity to others alongside God—for which He/She has not sent down any authority—and their place of shelter is the fire, and how calamitous that abode of those who do harm!

And, indeed, God did fulfill His/Her promise to you, when, by His/Her leave, you were about to destroy your foes—until the moment when you lost heart and disputing the command, in opposition, withdrew, even after He/She had brought you within sight of that for which you were longing. There are among you some who yearn for this world, just as there are among you some who yearn for the other world. And so, He/She prevented you from defeating your challengers, so that He/She might put you to the test. But now He/She has cleared your error in forgiveness, for Divine Reality is limitless in the bestowal of Its bounty to the faithful.

(Remember) when you fled, paying attention to no one, even while behind you the Messenger was calling to you, whereupon He/She gave you affliction, in return for affliction, so that you should learn not to grieve over what had fallen through your hands, nor what had happened to you; for Divine Reality is well aware of all that you do.

And (remember) how, after this distress, He/She sent down to you a sense of security—an inner calm enfolded some of you; while others, anxious for themselves, wandered in confused thinking about God—with suspicions due to ignorance—saying, "Did we have any power of decision at all?" Say, "Truly, all power of decision rests with God." They try to conceal within themselves that which they would not wish to reveal to you, saying, "If we had had any power of decision, we would not have left so many dead behind." Respond: "Even if you had remained in your homes, those whose death had been ordained would have gone forth to the places where they were destined to lie down." And this so that Divine Reality might put to the test all that you hold within your chests, and render pure of any dross your innermost hearts, for God knows well what is within hearts.

Behold, as for those of you who turned away on the day the two hosts met—it was Satan (the arrogant, misleading ego within) that caused them to stumble, by means of something they had done (that opened the door). But now Divine Reality has erased your errors, in forgiveness. Truly, God is Much Forgiving, the Most Forbearing [*al-Ghafur, al-Halim*].

O you who have faith, do not be like those who deny the Truth and say of their brothers who set out on a journey across the earth or go to war, "If they had but remained with us, they wouldn't have died," or "they wouldn't have been killed"—for God will cause such thoughts to be a source of bitter regret in their hearts, for it is Divine Reality that bestows life and grants death. And God sees all that you do.

And truly, if you are slain or die in God's Way, then surely forgiveness from God and His/Her Compassion [*Rahmat*] is better than any fortune one might amass in this world.

For truly, if you die or are killed, it will surely be into Divine Reality that you are gathered.

And it is from God's Compassion that you softened towards them, for if you had been harsh or hard of heart, they would have broken away from you; so pardon them, and pray that they be forgiven. And consult them regarding matters of community concern; then when you have decided on a course of action, put your trust in

God; for truly, Divine Reality loves those who place their trust in It [*inna Allaha yuhibbu al-mutawakkileen*].

If Divine Reality supports you, nothing can overcome you, but if Divine Reality were to forsake you, who indeed after that could come to your aid? In Divine Reality then, let the faithful put their trust.

And no Prophet could be false to his trust—since he who deceives must fully face his deceit on the Day of Standing, when every soul shall be fulfilled in whatever he or she has sought, and none shall be wronged.

Is then one who strives after God's good pleasure like one who has drawn towards himself or herself the reproach of Divine Reality and whose refuge is the raging fire?—how terrible a journey's end.

In God's sight, they are on different levels; for God sees all that they do.

Truly, God favored the faithful when He/She raised up a Messenger from among themselves, conveying His/Her Signs to them, encouraging their growth in purity, and teaching them the Divine Book and wisdom, when before they had clearly been lost in confusion.

And now that a calamity has befallen you, after you had inflicted twice as much, do you ask yourselves, "How has this happened?" Say: "It results from your own selves." Truly, God has the power to will anything;

and all that transpired on the day when the two hosts met in battle happened by God's leave, in order that He might determine the faithful,

and determine those who were poisoned with hypocrisy and, when they were told, "Come, fight in God's Cause," or "Defend yourselves," answered, "If we had known how to fight, we would have followed you." On that day, they were nearer to ungrateful denial than faith, uttering with their mouths what was not in their hearts, while Divine Reality knew well what they were trying to conceal.

They who held back said of their brothers, "Had they but listened to us, they would not have been killed." Say: "Avert death from yourselves then, if what you say is true."

But do not think of those killed in the Way of God as dead. No! They are alive. With their Sustainer they have their sustenance,

delighting in that which their Sustainer has granted them out of His/Her Bounty. And they rejoice in the glad tidings given to those left behind who have not yet joined them—that they need have no fear, neither shall they grieve.

They rejoice in the glad tidings of the blessings and abundance of Divine Reality and that Divine Reality will not fail to recompense the faithful—

those who respond to the call of Divine Reality and the Messenger even after affliction has befallen them. For those who persevere in doing the beautiful and remain conscious of Divine Reality, for them is a magnificent recompense.

People warned them, "See how a great army has gathered against you," to frighten them. But this only increased their faith, so that they responded, "God is sufficient for us; and how excellent He/She is as Guardian of All Our Affairs!" [*HasbunAllahu wani'ma al-Wakil.*]

And they returned with God's blessings and bounty, with no harm touching them, for they had been striving for the good pleasure of God [*ridwana Allahi*]; and limitless is Divine Reality in Its great bounty.

It is only Satan (the obstinately perverse, scattered

one) who instills fear in you of those who are near to him, but do not be afraid of them; be in awe of Me, if you are of the station of those who trust.

And do not be grieved by those who hasten with others to deny Truth; surely, they can never harm Divine Reality. It is the will of God that they shall have no share of the sufficiency of the Hereafter, and tremendous anguish is theirs.

Truly, those who have traded faith for denial can never harm God, but it is they who experience great anguish.

And they should not imagine—those who insist on denying Truth—that Our giving them respite is good for them. We allow them to enjoy life as they will, but it only allows them further error; and shameful anguish is theirs.

(O you who are in denial) God would not abandon the faithful to your way of life, and so He/She will distinguish the harmful from the good. It is not His/Her will to give you insight into that which is beyond the reach of human perception, but God chooses whom He/She wills from among His/Her Messengers. Trust then, in Divine Reality and Its Messengers, for if you trust, and are conscious of Him/Her, yours is a magnificent recompense.

And they should not think—they who stubbornly withhold the gifts that Divine Reality has granted them from Its bounty—that that is good for them; no, it is harmful for them. That to which they cling so selfishly will, on the Day of Standing, be bound around their necks. For to God belongs the inheritance of the heavens and the earth, and Divine Reality is aware of all that you do.

God has heard the speech of those who have said, "See how God is in need, and we are rich, without need." We shall record what they have said, as well as their killing of the prophets, against all that is right. And We shall say, "Taste suffering through fire

in return for what your own hands have wrought; for never does Divine Reality cause any wrong to one who serves."

And as for those who claim, "Behold, God has bidden us not to trust in any Messenger unless he comes to us with offerings flamed by fire (from heaven)." Say: "Even before me, there came to you Messengers with all evidence of the Truth, as well as with what you mention—why then did you kill them, if what you say is true?"

And if they reject you, even so, before your time other Messengers have been denied, even when they came with Clear Signs, and with Books of Divine Wisdom, and with light-giving Revelation.

Every soul shall have a taste of death. Only on the Day of Standing (before God) are you recompensed in full; then he or she who is drawn away from the fire and enters into paradise will have attained felicity. For the life of this world is but enjoyment of self-deception.

You will most certainly be tried in your possessions and in your own selves; and, indeed, you shall hear much that will cause you grief from those to whom Revelation was granted before your time, as well as from those who have come to attribute divinity to others beside God. But if you patiently persevere and remain conscious of *Hu*— see how this is something upon which to set one's heart.

And behold, God accepted a solemn pledge from those who were gifted Revelation before: "Clearly make it known to humankind, and do not conceal it." But they threw it behind their backs and traded it for a miserable gain; how calamitous is their trade.

Do not think that those who revel in what they have contrived, and who love to be praised for what they have not done, don't think that they can escape anguish, for theirs is grievous suffering.

For to God belongs the dominion over the heavens and the earth; and God has power over all things. [*Walillahi mulku as-samawati wal-ardi wallahu a'ala kulli shay-in qadeer.*]

Truly, in the creation of the heavens and the earth, and in the alternation of night and day, there are indeed Signs for all who are endowed with tender insight,

those who remember God [*allazheena yazhkuruna Allah*, those who *zhikr* "Allah"] standing, and sitting, and when they lie down to sleep, and contemplate creation—of the heavens and the earth: "O our Sustainer! You have not created this without meaning and purpose! Limitless are You in Your subtle glory! Protect us from the anguish of the fire!

"O our Sustainer! Whomever You admit to the fire You cover with disgrace; such wrong-doers will have none to aid them.

"O our Sustainer, behold, we heard a voice calling to faith: 'Trust in your Sustainer!' And we came to trust. O our Sustainer, forgive us, then, our faults, and clear our harmful deeds, and take to Yourself our souls, in fulfillment, that we might be gathered among the righteous.

"And O our Sustainer, grant us that which You have promised us through Your Messengers, and do not let us be disgraced on the Day of Standing (before You). Truly You never fail to fulfill Your Promise."

And thus does their Sustainer answer their prayer: "Never shall I allow to be lost the labor of any one of you who labors, whether male or female: you are each

parts, one of another. Those who have left their homes
or been driven out from them, or suffered difficulty on
My Way, or struggled or been slain, truly, I will put right
their wrongs, and admit them to gardens beneath which
rivers flow—a recompense from the Presence of God,
and from His/Her Presence is the most beautiful of
recompense [*thawaban min 'indi Allahi, wa Allahu 'indahu
husnu ath-thawab*]."

Do not let the strutting about of the deniers through
the land deceive you.

It is but a brief pleasure, but their abode is the
burning fire—what a terrible place of rest.

While those who are conscious of their Sustainer, for
them are gardens, with rivers flowing through, within
which they abide—a gift (a "station," *manzil* given,
nazulan) from the Presence of Divine Reality, and that
which is within the Presence of God is the best for those
who are true and good [*'inda Allahi khayrun lil-abrar*].

And there are, certainly, among the People of the
Book, those who trust in Divine Reality, in the Revelation
to you, and in the Revelation to them, bowing in humility
before Divine Reality; they will not trade the Signs of
God for a trifling gain. For them is a reward with their
Sustainer, and Divine Reality is swift in reckoning.

O you who have come to faith! Persevere in patience,
and keep striving with one another in patience, and
keep your connection, and remain conscious of Divine
Reality, so that you might truly attain felicity. [*Ya ayyuha
al-lazheena amanu, asbiru, wa saabiru, wa raabitu, wattaqu
Allaha, la'allakum tuflihuun.*]

Camille Adams Helminski has been a student of the Qur'an for more than forty years. Co-Director of the Threshold Society (sufism.org), she has long been dedicated to facilitating direct personal experience of the Divine.

She is the first woman to render a significant portion of the Quran into English with her heart-opening *The Light of Dawn, Daily Readings of the Holy Qur'an*, originally published twenty-three years ago. She has created two anthologies based in Qur'anic inspiration, one in honor of all the beauties of the natural world and our responsibility of stewardship, *The Book of Nature: A Sourcebook of Spiritual Perspectives on Nature and the Environment*, and a companion volume, *The Book of Character: An Anthology of Writings on Virtue from Islamic and Other Sources*, both published by the Book Foundation.

She is the author of numerous other books, including the now classic *Women of Sufism, A Hidden Treasure, Writings and Stories of Mystic Poets, Scholars, and Saints*, which has helped to increase awareness of the integral contribution of women to the spiritual path of Islam. Long immersed in the traditions of the Way of Mevlana Jalaluddin Rumi, she has also collaborated in the translation of the classic works of the tradition: *Rumi's Sun: The Teachings of Shams of Tabriz* (selections from the *Maqalat*); *Rumi and His Friends, Stories of the Lovers of God* (selections from the *Menaqib al-Arifin*); and together with her husband, Kabir, many volumes of Rumi's poetry. In 2021 she completed *The Way of Mary: Maryam Beloved of God*, which through a journey with the life of Beloved Mary, drawn from Jewish, Christian, and Islamic sources, illuminates our Oneness in Spirit.

This *Volume I* is the first in a series of eleven volumes, God willing, which together are intended to hold the complete one hundred and fourteen *surahs* of the Holy Qur'an. We offer this translation to support the increased opening of our awareness to all the Compassionate Generosity and Loving Guidance of the Divine Bestowal—that Love that is always communicating with us, which we simply need to open our hearts to hear, and our eyes to see.

Made in United States
North Haven, CT
01 April 2023